PLAYING RUDOLF HESS

BY

NICHOLAS KINSEY

Printed in the United States of America

Second Edition, October 2023
ISBN: 978-1-7381687-2-9

Cinegrafica Films & Publishing
820 Rougemont
Quebec, QC G1X 2M5
Canada
Tel. 418-652-3345

In memory of my mother
Winifred Mary Pryce

FOREWORD

This novel is an imaginative re-creation of a true story: the investigation of the Rudolf Hess imposter by Britain's Secret Services during WWII. I have tried to stick to the facts as we know them. The events, dates and locations are accurate. The story features two very mismatched characters: the quiet and self-effacing Hess, highly educated, from a middle class Bavarian family who was called the "conscience of the Nazi Party" and, like his friend Hitler, was a vegetarian, fastidious about food and natural remedies, with a love of tennis and flying; and the other Hess, the deplorable prisoner No. 7 — as Hess was known at Spandau Prison in Berlin — who couldn't get the simplest facts of his existence straight, had never played tennis and was no vegetarian, shovelling his food into his mouth and displaying terrible table manners. The latter was known in wartime intelligence services as the "phoney Hess", according to the retired MI6 officer, Charles Fraser-Smith.

But people today don't always believe what they see in front of them. After a massive amount of physical evidence confirmed the existence of an imposter, came the bombshell in January 2019 when the New Scientist published the results of a DNA test on a blood sample belonging to prisoner no. 7 and a member of the Hess family. The DNA evidence was suspect from the start when the remarkably well-preserved blood sample drawn from the prisoner in 1982 was submitted for testing in an Austrian lab and appeared to be fresh and only slightly degraded after more than thirty years. Furthermore, no one appears to know the origin of the sample, since there were no routine health checks of prisoners at Spandau back in the 1980s, and the Hess family maintained custody of all the samples during the testing. The most persistent evidence that prisoner no. 7 was a fraud came from the physical examinations of his body and his dental records.

"Hess looks crazy now. The sickest man one ever saw. Born to burn at any stake for any cause that happens to come along. He has a round, bald patch like a monk's on the top of his head. I gazed into those enormous black pupils, the eyes of a fanatic, cavernous in that emaciated, grey-white face."

Dame Laura Knight, journalist
Nuremberg, 1946

One

Berlin, September 1973

The roofs of old Berlin flashed by in bursts of light. An old man with a gaunt face and bushy eyebrows in a threadbare grey suit sat on a metal bench breathing in the blue sky and enjoying the warmth of the sun on his face, oblivious to his Soviet guards. It had been some 30 years since he felt that joyous and indefinable feeling of liberty, of life beating in his breast during long walks in the Welsh highlands with the wind blowing off the mountains. His hand shook as he struggled with his handcuffs to pull a pair of spectacles from his pocket, hoping to get a glimpse of his whereabouts in the city.

He was locked in the back of a green ambulance as it rushed through the back streets of the British Sector. The ambulance followed two motorcycle outriders with a Mercedes sedan carrying a Russian flag bringing up the rear.

Moments later, the ambulance swept into the courtyard of the British Military Hospital. A Soviet army major named Voitov jumped out of the Mercedes and went to the back of the ambulance, where he was joined by two soldiers. Voitov barked an order in Russian.

"Hurry up. Bring him out."

The soldiers pulled the old man out of the truck and followed Voitov into the building by the back door.

Inside the old baroque hall, they were met by a noisy crowd of hospital and diplomatic staff from the four Allied powers who quickly focussed their attention on the arrival of Rudolf Hess, the solitary prisoner of Spandau, coming up the stairs from the courtyard. Hess stumbled forward, dazzled by the bright lights and the welcoming faces. This was not his first time here. He had spent a good deal of time in this same hospital four years earlier for a perforated ulcer.

Colonel Philips, the director of the hospital, stepped forward and shook Voitov's hand.

"Good morning, Major Voitov. I hope the press aren't giving you a hard time."

Voitov looked at the crowd with distaste.

"Morning, Colonel. No, we come in through back door."

"I believe you know your colleagues."

A French general advanced to shake Voitov's hand.

"*Cher Major, il nous fait plaisir de vous revoir.*"

"*Merci, Général.*"

A US military attaché stepped forward.

"Hi, Major. I see you have the prisoner. What's his problem this time?"

Voitov frowned at this remark.

"We see what the doctors say, yes?"

Colonel Philips stepped closer.

"Major Voitov, we'd better move along. Please come with me, gentlemen."

Philips and Voitov led the old man into the reception hall, where he was placed on a hard chair in handcuffs, facing a long table with the senior medical staff of the four Allied nations. Military and diplomatic staff sat further back in the room.

The flags of France, Britain, the U.S. and the Soviet Union were on display. Off to the side there were tables laden with hors d'oeuvres and bottles of wine, whisky and vodka for the upcoming reception.

Dr Hugh Terry, the British physician responsible for the prisoner's medical examination, entered the room and went to the podium. He loudly clapped his hands together, asking for silence.

"Thank you for coming. I am Dr Hugh Terry and as you all know, the reason for the visit today is to check up on Mr Hess' general health and provide a full report to the Allied powers. Major Voitov, can we get rid of those handcuffs, please?"

Major Voitov rose from his chair and scowled at Terry and his colleagues.

"No comfort, sir."

Dr Fabre, the French physician, stood up, as did the American, Dr Leno.

"*S'il vous plait, Major. Pas de menottes, c'est un vieil homme.* No handcuffs, he's an old man."

"Yes, let's have those handcuffs off," Leno said.

Voitov finally relented and barked an order in Russian to a guard standing nearby.

"Off with the handcuffs."

The guard approached the old man and unlocked the cuffs. Hess rubbed his wrists to get the circulation going and looked around gratefully.

"*Vielen Dank.*"

Leno could see the angry red lines marking Hess' wrists and felt disgusted. He glared at Voitov, but the Russian ignored him.

Terry turned to talk to the patient.

"How are you feeling today, Mr Hess?"

"*Gut, sehr gut.*"

"Do you have any complaints?"

Hess shifted his weight uncomfortably and shot a timorous glance at Voitov.

"My books, my papers. They are all gone."

Major Voitov stared straight ahead, showing no sign of having heard the prisoner.

"I mean your health, sir," Terry said. "Faintness of breath, stomach ailments, headaches, anything?"

"No, I am fine."

Terry watched Hess squirm in his seat, looking uncomfortable just as a British nurse clutching a thin cushion stood up and walked briskly towards the prisoner.

"Stop!" Voitov ordered.

The two Russian guards stepped forward, brandishing their submachine guns and barred the way. The nurse stopped in her tracks, frightened.

"I think he needs a cushion," the nurse murmured.

"No comforts!" Voitov said, turning to Terry. "Please. This man is a prisoner. It is against the Nuremberg agreement."

The nurse returned silently to her seat as Leno stood up.

"Oh, come on, Major," Leno said. "Let's not make a scene."

"*Pitié, Major,*" Fabre said, siding with Leno.

Voitov scowled at Fabre and Leno.

"It is against the spirit of the convention. Please try to remember that."

"Any other questions?" Terry asked the fractious crowd, trying to move things along.

Leno stood up.

"You had a perforated ulcer four years ago. Have you any complaints since, Mr Hess?"

4

"No, sir. I am well, but I have no exercise now. No more walking in the garden."

Terry turned to Fabre.

"Any questions, Dr Fabre?"

"*Vous n'avez plus d'appétit, Monsieur Hess?* You look very thin. Have you lost weight?"

"*Vielleicht,*" said Hess, nodding.

There was an unruly murmuring in the room among the Allied medical staff, many disapproving of Hess' conditions of detention.

"Well, thank you everyone," Thomas said. "I think we can now proceed with our tests. First the eye test with Dr Dowson and then the barium meal and X-rays. Mr Hess, have you anything else to add?"

"*Nein, danke.*"

As the crowd moved towards the drinks table, Hess was led out of the hall by the two Russian guards.

Dr Dowson, a kindly older man in a white lab coat, completed the eye tests with Hess in the ophthalmology department. He then walked Hess down to the X-ray room where Dr Terry, the radiologist Major Bill Leach and his assistant Sergeant MacLean were waiting for the patient.

"I will have the glasses sent to you, Mr Hess," Dr Dowson said. "Don't use the old ones. They are worse than useless. Good day, sir."

Hess nodded gratefully at Dowson as young Major Leach stepped forward to greet him.

"Over here, Mr Hess. Please put on the white shift, then you will have the barium. Sergeant MacLean will assist you."

As MacLean and Hess left the room to prepare for the X-ray

tests, Terry went over to talk with Dowson.

"So Dr Dowson, anything else to report?"

"You know, at his age, it is quite normal to have retinal disorders. He suffers from dry eyes, itching and redness, but his sight is still quite good."

In the reception room, Major Voitov stood in a group of employees from the Soviet diplomatic mission under surveillance by a handful of KGB operatives. The party was going well with the French and the Soviets sticking to their own while the Americans and British mingled. Voitov had a smile on his face as he looked around the room, knocking back several vodkas from passing trays of drinks.

For the major, his posting as the Russian governor of Spandau was a dream come true. For three months of the year, he was in charge of one prisoner held in an empty prison with all the delights of West Berlin accessible nearby. The four powers took turns guarding the prisoner, all paid for by the German government from the occupation budget. Major Voitov had 37 soldiers under his command manning six towers around the prison. If ever there was a plum assignment in the Soviet military, this was it.

Voitov knew that there was a movement to free Hess among the Western Allies, but the Soviet authorities loved their foothold in West Berlin and weren't ready to give it up for any humanitarian argument in favour of Hess.

In the X-ray room, Dr Leach laid several large transparencies on the viewing screen for Terry, Fabre, Leno and two Soviet medical professionals.

"The duodenum shows some scarring here, but I don't see any tumours."

Leno looked closely at the X-ray.

"Yes, it looks good. What about the small intestine?"

"I'll get to that. Any further comments, gentlemen?"

Fabre and Leno pulled back to allow the Soviet medical people to get a better look. The Soviets grunted their approval and Leach pulled down the X-ray, clipping a new one of the small intestine to the viewing screen.

Dr Terry stepped into the noisy reception room and went over to talk to Colonel Philips.

"The X-rays are normal, sir. We are doing a final check."

"Good, good. Voitov is not giving you any trouble?"

"Prima facie arsehole, sir."

Philips laughed and downed his whisky.

"Poor Connie had quite a scare there. She was very upset, all because of those damned Russkies."

"Yes, sir."

"The major was enjoying himself. He is old NKVD, a strong believer in pain and suffering and putting a bullet in the back of your head."

"I agree the Russians are making life as uncomfortable as they can for Hess. I've got to go back, sir."

Philips nodded as Terry left.

In the X-ray room, Dr Leach stuck his head around the corner and called to Hess.

"Pictures are good, Mr Hess. You can get dressed now. Thank you for your patience."

7

PLAYING RUDOLF HESS

Dr Terry watched as Hess returned to the changing cubicle in the corner of the room and started to get dressed. He quickly removed the white shift, sliding it away from his body and down his arms. For a few moments, the man was naked as he reached backwards, feeling for the sleeve of his shirt.

Terry approached to get a look at the old man's bony chest. He noticed two small linear scars and a scar on his wrist, but no evidence of major scarring on his chest. As Terry helped Hess into his shirt, he wondered what had happened to Hess' war wounds. The man had been wounded three times during the war: once by shrapnel in the left hand and upper arm in France in 1916 and twice in Romania in 1917 with an injury to his left arm in July and a very severe chest wound in August that left him hospitalized for four months.

"*Es tut mir Leid, Herr Hess.* I am sorry to ask you this," Terry said to the old man. "But what happened to your war wounds? I can't see any trace of them."

Hess' cheerful demeanour changed instantly. His face became a chalk-white mask while his body began to shake uncontrollably. He hurried to button up his shirt as he looked at Thomas in shock.

"I saw your military file. You were wounded in the left lung in Romania in 1917. Severely wounded, sir. Where are your scars?"

Hess looked down, avoiding Terry's gaze and then muttered: "*Zu spät, zu spät* (Too late, too late)."

"A large calibre bullet punched a hole in your left lung and would have exited through your back. I see no trace of such a wound, Herr Hess. Can you please explain, sir?"

Terry was suddenly concerned that the man might be having a heart attack and stood back to let him pass as Hess shuffled across the room toward the bathroom. At the last

8

moment, he turned to look at Terry and was about to say something when a flood of barium and diarrhoea discharged onto the floor.

MacLean appeared in the doorway.

"Mr Hess, sir, are you alright?"

Looking severely distressed, Hess disappeared into the bathroom without a word.

MacLean turned to Terry.

"What happened, sir?"

"I wouldn't know, Sergeant."

Two

England 1973

Paul Cummings wore an old cardigan and checked shirt as he watered the flowers in the garden of a semi-detached house in Surrey when his buxom German-born wife Claudia popped her head out the kitchen door.

"Telephone, Paul. I think it is the office."

Nearing retirement with a closely clipped moustache and thinning hair, Paul frowned, turning away from his beloved flower beds.

"Bloody hell. What do they want on a Sunday?"

"Do you want to ring them back?"

Paul dropped the hose and headed back towards the house to turn off the tap.

"No, I'll take it."

Paul entered the kitchen, where Claudia was cleaning vegetables in the sink. Paul picked up the wall phone.

"Hello."

Paul listened for a time, looking at his wife. Now in her fifties, Claudia was still quite attractive, with her green eyes and greying hair.

"Yes, sir."

Paul put the phone down.

"What is it?"

"There's been a crisis with Max. They want me on the 4 o'clock flight to Berlin."

"Max. Can't he leave you in peace?"

"Something's happened. This seems to be a bit more serious. I should be back in a few days."

Claudia put down the kitchen knife and stepped towards her husband embracing him.

"You better be back. They are giving you a going-away party on Friday. You earned it. Next month they can send someone else. You'll be out of it."

There was a wistful look in Paul's eyes as he reflected on his retirement.

"I have put in quite a few years, haven't I?"

"No one has given as much as you, *Liebling*."

"I will miss you, darling."

"No, you bloody won't," Claudia said laughing. "Berlin is nice at this time of year. You will be visiting with old friends, catching up on gossip and getting free drinks at all your favourite bars."

"You know I have always loved Berlin," Paul replied grinning at his wife.

Berlin 1973

Dr Terry in a white lab coat, was in conversation with a colleague as he arrived at his office in the British Military hospital. He took leave of the man near the door and then stepped inside, noticing a stranger in a dark suit and raincoat who sat quietly in a chair opposite his desk.

"Can I help you, sir? My secretary is on her lunch hour."
Paul Cummings stood up.

"Dr Terry, I presume?"

"Yes. Why don't you come back later and my secretary will fix you up with an appointment?"

Terry turned to remove his lab coat as Cummings dropped a brown envelope on the desk and went to close the door. Terry suddenly looked alarmed.

"What is this? Who are you?"

From the cut of the suit and the raincoat he wore, Terry thought that his unannounced visitor must be military or embassy staff. Cummings gave the doctor a knowing smile.

"I think you should sit down and take a look at the photographs. They are rather well done, you know. A long lens on a sunny day."

Terry picked up the envelope from the desk and removed six 8x10, black and white glossies.

"That looks a bit like you, doesn't it sport? You were chatting with a British serviceman at Spandau. A good friend, perhaps?"

The top photograph showed the doctor talking to a British guard at the Spandau prison gate.

"I don't know what this has got to do with anything."

"Oh, come on, Dr Terry. This is not the first time you were seen talking to this young man. We reckon the Soviets and the Americans have their own set by now and are starting to wonder about you."

"Who are you?"

"Serving her Majesty, just like you."

"You're some kind of spook, aren't you? I've seen your type in Northern Ireland."

"I am afraid my identity must remain a secret. So are we

going to have a nice chat over lunch or do I have to arrest you and haul your arse in handcuffs down to the embassy in full view of your colleagues?"

Terry was rendered speechless. He removed his white lab coat and put on his suit coat as Cummings collected the photographs and followed him out of the office.

Three

The sun was shining as Dr Terry and Paul Cummings walked through the Berlin Großer Tiergarten park as lunch hour strollers were heading back to work.

"Lovely day, Doctor. I do love this park. You know it had a hard time during the war. It lost all its trees during the Allied bombardment and after the war, it was turned into temporary farmland for growing potatoes and vegetables. But we are not here to talk about the Tiergarten, are we? So why don't you tell me what you were doing stalking one of our prison warders at Spandau?"

"This is quite ridiculous. I have known Henry for years. We went to the same prep school. He works several months a year at Spandau and recently has been in direct contact with Rudolf Hess."

"And what prompted your interest in our famous Nazi war criminal?"

"Look, I was in charge of Hess' medical examination about a month ago. He was having a series of X-rays done to determine whether his intestinal tract was functioning properly. He had a perforated duodenal ulcer several years ago."

"Yes, I remember that time. There was a flurry of diplomatic messages back and forth with the Soviets and the Americans."

"He is lucky to be alive today. I was simply asking Henry to keep me posted as to his medical condition, that's all."

"So Henry was giving you an unofficial progress report on the old man?"

"Well, that's not quite true."

Dr Terry and Cummings arrived at a *biergarten* near the water. They sat at a table away from the lunchtime crowd. The waiter brought Cummings a stein of Berliner Weisse beer and a coffee for his companion. Cummings took his glass and drank deeply, leaving froth on his upper lip.

"Look, I had a chance to examine Hess and I have serious doubts as to his identity."

"And what put you on this track, Doctor?"

"The man should have a whopping great hole in his chest, both in the front and back. I have seen his army medical records at the Berlin document centre."

Cummings drank his beer in silence.

"The medical record shows that he was wounded in France in 1916 in the left hand and upper arm and then twice in Romania in 1917. The wound in France was superficial, but the wound in Romania was an almost fatal lung shot."

"Are you sure you don't want a beer, Doctor?"

"No thanks. I have seen this kind of damage to bone and tissue in Northern Ireland. A gunshot like that leaves awful scars. We are talking about a large calibre bullet, probably 7.62 mm. Whoever this man is in Spandau, he is not Rudolf Hess."

"I wouldn't know, Doctor, but I do think you may be overstepping your authority investigating the prisoner and expressing your opinion on this matter."

"This is not an opinion, sir. It is a fact."

"I agree. It does sound troubling. Maybe the wound was only superficial, and the scar healed over. That could explain it."

"Not possible. We are talking major trauma, a lung perforation and the serious infection that followed. The scars are just not there."

"So you have made this a personal crusade: Henry, the document centre?"

"Well, I was curious. Who wouldn't be?"

"What are your intentions? Are you going to the press with this scoop?"

"Heavens, no. I hadn't thought of that."

"You know that Her Majesty's government has the nasty habit of gagging the press when it is a question of national security. I am not sure it would be wise to continue your research into the matter."

"National security! You can't be serious. What is your name?"

"You can call me Paul."

"OK, Paul. Call me Hugh. Hess is an imposter costing the German government £500,000 a year and making a laughing stock of the four Allied powers. Isn't it about time we heard the truth?"

"The Official Secrets Act has a long arm, Hugh."

"Are you warning me off, Paul?"

"Lord, no. I would never do such a thing. My job is to explain your curious behaviour to the British government and our American friends. I need to convince them that you aren't trading secrets with the Soviets."

Cummings took a long drink of beer and glanced around for anyone who might have them under surveillance - an old reflex during the Cold War.

"This is ridiculous. We are talking about a German national held in a German prison. The man should be released immediately. This has nothing to do with the Queen's dirty laundry or a bloody Philby-Maclean spook in Her Majesty's services."

"I hear you, Hugh. Of course, I agree with a lot of what you say, but make no mistake about it, Rudolf Hess is very much part of our national security and has been for 32 years."

Terry looked at Cummings with genuine surprise.

"During the war, Churchill made him an official secret."

"You must be joking."

"Hugh. Do I sound like I'm joking? If you continue your research on Hess, you'll bring down the long arm of the Official Secrets Act. That's all I'm saying. They will use any method at their disposal to stop you and they will, I guarantee it, ruin your life. Now, with your name on a case file, you have given them the means to get at you."

"Are you threatening me?"

"Of course not. I'm retiring from the service in a few weeks, so I won't be involved in bringing you down. The job will go to a lot of faceless people at London Central."

"You can't be serious."

"I am dead serious, Hugh. They can lock you up on any charge they like and say it is a national emergency."

Terry remained silent.

"You do understand? They will search your house and your past, and arrest you on trumped-up charges."

"Why Hess? Isn't he an open book?"

"Hess is a curious historical anomaly, Hugh. Why he became a national secret, I really don't know. You remember the Nuremberg trials."

17

"Of course, I do."

"Well, then you will remember that Hess was sent to that bombed-out shell of a city in October, 1946. I remember his interrogation. Colonel John Amen was chief interrogator for US forces and he went at him tooth and nail."

Four

Nuremberg 1945

In an office of the old German *Justizpalast*, Hess sat manacled to a chair in his old Luftwaffe uniform under a bright light. In the shadows behind a desk sat Colonel John H. Amen, a no-nonsense, heavy-jowled military intelligence expert with bushy eyebrows and a receding hairline who worked as a special assistant to the US special prosecutor Justice Robert Jackson. Near him sat a court reporter, an interpreter and an American psychologist, Dr Gilbert, a small man with round spectacles and slicked back hair. The immensely fat *Reichsmarschall* Hermann Göring, clad in a pearl-grey uniform, stepped into the light illuminating the prisoner's face.

"Don't you know me?"

Hess looked up slowly at the *Reichsmarschall*.

"You are Herr Göring. I have seen you in the prison."

"We have been together for years."

Hess lifted his manacled hand in a helpless gesture.

"You don't recognize me?"

"Not personally, but I know your name."

"Listen, Hess. Stop it. You know very well that I was the

supreme commander of the Luftwaffe. You flew to Britain in one of my planes. You must remember?"

"I have no recollection."

"Don't you remember that I was made a *Reichsmarschall* at a meeting of the *Reichstag* at which you were present?"

Hess looked confused.

"Do you not recall that the Führer on another occasion announced that if anything happened to him, I would be his successor; and that if anything happened to me, you were to be my successor? We talked about it for a long time afterwards."

"I cannot remember," Hess said.

"You must remember Herr Messerschmitt. You were well acquainted with him. He designed all our fighter planes. And he gave you the plane that I refused to give you, the plane you flew to Britain in. Messerschmitt gave it to you behind my back."

Hess shook his head, infuriating the *Reichsmarshall* who was ushered out of the room by a guard. An old man by the name of Karl Haushofer was immediately brought in, stepping into the bright light.

"*Oh, mein Gott.* You are so thin and..."

"Pardon me, sir, who are you?"

Haushofer looked flabbergasted.

"Rudolf, don't you recognize me? I am Karl Haushofer, Professor Haushofer. You remember me?"

"Are we on first-name terms?"

"We have called each other by our first names for twenty years. I saw your wife and child. They are well."

Haushofer grabbed Hess' free hand.

"May I shake your hand? You have a wonderful boy. He is seven years old now. I have seen him. Your wife and son look forward to seeing you."

Tears of joy filled the old professor's eyes as he looked at his protégé.

"I was sent to Dachau after your flight and my son Heinz was arrested. You remember my son Albrecht, who served you faithfully. He was my eldest. He is dead now."

"The doctors tell me that my memory will come back to me," Hess replied. "And then I will recognize an old friend again. I am terribly sorry."

"I look in your eyes because for 22 years I have read in your eyes. I now see a little bit of recognition coming back to you. You remember the view of the Zugspitze mountain, the branches of the tree that hung so low? You must remember Heimbach, where you lived for so long."

As Haushofer retreated from the light and was taken away, Colonel Amen stood up and came around the desk. In the shadows, Paul Cummings in plainclothes leaned against the far wall, watching the colonel interrogate the prisoner.

"You remember Haushofer and Göring, don't you?"

"No, no. I do not remember them."

"You believe what they say?" Amen asked.

"I have no reason to believe that Germans do not tell the truth."

"Do you think all Germans tell the truth?"

"Yes. All the Germans I know," Hess replied.

"I could bring in a lot of Germans who won't tell you the truth," Amen said.

"You are talking about criminals."

"Such as Göring, for example."

"Obviously, I did not mean that."

"Well, is Göring a criminal?"

"Yes, a war criminal."

"How do you know what kind of criminal he is?"

"Because he is the same kind of criminal as me."

Raising his voice, Amen stepped very close to Hess and regarded him with a cynical air.

"I'm asking you, Mr Hess. How do you know he's not a pickpocket or a thief?"

"I am convinced that neither pickpockets nor thieves or others of that ilk are elevated to high office. Not in Germany, at least."

Fed up, Amen signalled to the guards to take the prisoner away.

Five

Berlin 1973

"Didn't it occur to Colonel Amen and his people, that this man was incapable of having known Göring and Haushofer?" Terry asked as Cummings examined the menu and wondered whether lunch would be a good idea.

Cummings put down the menu and looked at Terry.

"Ever hear the phrase 'character is destiny'?"

"No," Terry said frowning.

"You know, a person's character is the sum total of their dispositions to act. No one can give it to you or take it away. What you do is what you are."

Terry looked around impatiently, showing little interest in the conversation.

"That comes from Heraclitus, the Greek philosopher," Cummings said. "Amen's interrogation showed the character of Hess, his determination, his perseverance."

"He is an imposter and you know it."

"Hess was the mad monk of Nuremberg. He wanted to be there, to participate in the trial of the century, to be on the world stage. No one forced him to be there."

Terry reflected on the plethora of motives, all seemingly

contradictory when you assumed that Hess was an imposter.

"Listen to me a moment," Cummings continued. "Nuremberg was a military tribunal, a highly visible show trial with the victors sitting in judgement on the losers."

Terry looked at his watch.

"You may remember the Soviet prosecutors even tried to pin their own crimes on the German defendants: the 1943 Katyn massacre of Polish officers. During their advance east, the Wehrmacht discovered the mass graves of some 20,000 Poles and told the world about it, but no one believed them."

"Yes, I remember that."

"People have called Nuremberg a sanctimonious fraud. They are right. It was nothing but a show trial. Absolutely nobody at Nuremberg cared about the identity of the men in the box. Hess was a recognized Nazi war criminal and was going to be hanged. Justice was going to be served."

"Look, I better be going. I need to get back to my patients." Terry stood up ready to leave.

"Sit down, Doctor. I had all your appointments cancelled for the afternoon. I gave the excuse of an urgent meeting at the Embassy to your secretary."

Terry looked at Cummings with increasing annoyance.

"Sit down, relax and have a beer. You are free for the afternoon and I have a very interesting story to tell you."

Terry sat down in an angry silence.

"I started working as an agent in our intelligence services during the summer of 1940 after the surrender of France. Fear of German spies was all over the media at the time with the German invasion of Britain looming. Police stations up and down the country were being buried in reports of strangers, German-looking chaps and odd-looking characters. We had our hands full with what we called the invasion spies, that is

German agents who were coming ashore by boat or parachuting from aircraft to prepare the attack on Britain."

"My job in those days was to run off in the middle of the night to some small coastal town where a suspicious person had been arrested by the local constabulary and to ascertain whether the individual was actually a German agent, a case of amnesia or a patient escaping from an insane asylum."

England 1940

In the predawn stillness of the Kent coast agent Paul Cummings and a colleague sat in a car awaiting the arrival of a German spy near a copse of trees on a farmer's track. An intense-looking young man with striking features, Cummings was dressed in a dark suit and raincoat. The agents were looking for several spies who had arrived by dinghy after being dropped off by a trawler near Dungeness, Kent.

One of the spies, a man named Meier, had stumbled into a pub and ordered a drink in the morning before the opening hour. This had led to Meier being taken down to the local police station where he was promptly arrested and was now in MI5 custody. Meier had revealed the existence of a partner Waldberg who was still on the run and had been using emergency codes to communicate a pickup location to his German handlers.

Cummings and his colleague soon noticed a man hiding in a ditch slowly making his way towards the main road near an apple orchard.

Cummings signalled to his partner to come in behind the man cutting off any possibility of escape. Cummings waited for the officer to get into position before he approached the man with his Webley revolver drawn.

"*Hände hoch!*" Cummings yelled.

Waldberg, startled by the order, instantly raised his hands.

"*Guten Tag,* Herr Waldberg. We know who you are. We have been expecting you."

Waldberg looked downcast as Cummings and his colleague quickly arrested him along with his radio and other incriminating evidence in a lightweight bag.

Six

Berlin 1973

"As it turned out, Waldberg had been an Abwehr agent before the war and was the ringleader of the group called the 'Brussels spies' including Meier, Pons and Kiebaum," Cummings said. "All four were tried in the Old Bailey for espionage and three of them were later hanged. It was a political decision. The government at the time wanted to set an example."

"How many German spies were actually hanged during the war?"

"Not that many. Despite the clamour to have all spies executed after the Treachery Act was passed by parliament in 1940, spies were kept active and used to pass controlled information back to their handlers. Suspects were interrogated and offered the opportunity to collaborate with our services or face execution. Most enemy agents chose to collaborate and were kept active, working as double agents for Britain."

"I remember hearing about the double-cross system used during the war," Terry said.

"Well, then you know how effective it was in deceiving the enemy. Our job was to take charge of the double agents and help them with money, lodging, and wireless communications with their German handlers. It was all organized by the Twenty (the XX) Committee under John Masterman, who wrote the scripts for each of the double agents and provided the deception material. For most of us, it was actually very boring work babysitting these characters in safe houses around London, since many of these chaps were crazy nutters or sociopaths."

Cummings sipped his beer.

"All of this came to an end for me in May 1941 when I received a call from my old boss, Major Frank Foley, who I had worked with in Berlin before the war."

Scotland, May 10, 1941

A Messerschmitt Bf110 flew over the coast, coming off the North Sea near Holy Island in Northumberland in the late evening light. The plane dived, picking up speed until it was racing at some 300 mph over the hills and hedgerows. In the fields, there were labourers finishing their work and returning home.

In the cockpit, Hess held a map firmly in one hand and steered with the other. He headed northwest towards the west coast of Scotland near Kilmarnock, south of Glasgow, flying over Dungavel house, the home of the Duke of Hamilton. He continued on reaching the sea before turning south along the coast. He spotted a towering rock rising out of the sea just off the mainland and, using this as a landmark, turned inland. After a while, he slipped the map into his flying suit and climbed to an altitude of some 6,500 feet. He switched off the engines and opened the canopy. He tried to climb out with a parachute strapped to his back, but the wind and air pressure pushed him back. The aircraft was now losing altitude fast. He struggled, trying to extricate himself as the plane headed into a downward spiral towards the earth.

A farmer who was unloading hay for his cows near Eaglesham, south of Glasgow, looked up to see the Messerschmitt race by overhead and crash in a field nearby, followed by a fireball. He ran towards the plane and the pilot hobbling towards him from across the field.

"Who are you?"

"Ich bin Hauptmann Alfred Horn."

"You are German?"

"Yes, sir. I am here to see the Duke of Hamilton."

"Blimey, you're a German spy."

The farmer held up his pitchfork in a threatening manner as Hess put his hands on his head.

"I want to go to Dungavel House. I have an important message for the Duke of Hamilton."

The farmer looked at his prisoner in disbelief.

It was dark at the Maryhill Barracks in Glasgow as a military jeep pulled up at the gate. There was no one in the guardhouse on a Saturday night, so the jeep drove through, stopping near the barracks and honking its horn. Constable Williamson emerged from the jeep followed by Hess limping badly, with Constable Smith bringing up the rear with his Webley revolver.

The two constables accompanied Hess into a large room as a guard in shirtsleeves and braces arrived. Williamson looked at the half-dressed man with disdain.

"Fuckin' eejits. You might want to put a man on the gate,

keep out the German army."

The guard looked around sheepishly, glancing at the prisoner.

"Sorry, sir. Most of the men have the night off and are having a bit of a booze up down at the pub. Who's he?"

"He's a fuckin' Nazi airman, that's who he is," Williamson said, grinning at the guard. "He got his signals mixed up and crashed his plane before he got to the North Pole."

Major Barrie and Captain Donald appeared at the door.

"Hello, Constable. I just heard the news. I'm Major Barrie and this is Captain Donald."

"I'm Constable Williamson and this is Constable Smith, sir. Looks like it is going to be a long night for all of us."

Barrie looked Hess up and down with disbelief.

"What's a German airman want in Scotland?"

"I think he's looking for the Scottish honours, sir," Williamson said. "He wants our crown jewels, he does."

"What's his name?" Barrie asked.

"He says he's Hauptmann Horn. He wants to go to Dungavel House to see the Duke of Hamilton. Says he knows the man."

"Have you searched him?"

Williamson and Smith looked at each other.

"No, sir."

"Then let's do it. Get that flying suit off him."

Smith, assisted by Williamson, helped Hess off with his flying suit, revealing a brand new Luftwaffe uniform underneath. Smith went through the man's pockets, pulling out pictures, medicine vials, a hypodermic needle, and some business cards. Williamson removed the airman's Leica camera from around his neck.

"Do we have any personal identification?" Barrie asked.

Smith stepped forward with the pictures and business cards. Barrie looked at the photographs of Horn with a young boy.

"Hauptmann, where are your identity papers?"

"I left them in Germany, sir."

Williamson pulled a folded map from the airman's suit with a view of the North Sea and a crude drawing of Dungavel castle.

"Look at this."

"It's a map and there is Dungavel marked on it. My superiors are going to love this," Barrie said.

Captain Donald slipped Hess a magazine photograph of an ME 110.

"Hauptmann Horn, you are an airman. I would be honoured if you would sign this photograph for me."

Hess looked at Donald with surprise. He smiled and picked up Donald's fountain pen, signing Hauptmann Horn over the picture. There was something familiar about the Horn's face, but Donald thought the man in front of him was gaunt, hollow-cheeked, and pale compared to the famous Nazi *Reichsminister*.

"I may be imagining things, but you look a lot like Rudolf Hess. You're his spitting image. What do you think, Major?"

"I think he is a German spy," Barrie said. "I am wondering where his radio is and what his business is in Scotland."

Seven

In the empty infirmary Hess sat silently on the floor in a yoga-type posture of relaxation. Footsteps sounded in the hallway and the door swung open as Douglas Hamilton, also known as the Duke of Hamilton, stepped into the room accompanied by Major Barrie.

"We have a visitor for you, Hauptmann Horn."

Hess got to his feet with difficulty, limping on his right foot, and slipped on his Luftwaffe jacket.

"This is Wing Commander Hamilton, Hauptmann Horn," Barrie said. "He has come at your request."

Hess shook hands eagerly with the Duke who was a handsome aviator with piercing eyes and a doleful expression, famous for his flight over Mount Everest in 1933.

"Mr Horn, I am Wing Commander Hamilton. I heard you sprained your ankle and injured your back jumping out of your plane."

"Ja, ja. It was a fantastic flight, Commander. The Scottish coast is so beautiful in the sunlight. There were none of the dense clouds predicted in our German weather reports."

"You know you could have been shot down."

"I was worried, sir. I even thought of turning back. As I came in over the coast, it started to get misty so I flew low over the fields."

"You passed over the castle, Dungavel?"

"Yes, I flew over it and then on to the west coast. I thought it would be easy to jump but when I opened the canopy and tried to climb out, the air pressure pushed me back."

"You are lucky to be alive, sir. There are techniques for baling out of aircraft."

"I have good luck. Can we speak privately, sir?"

Hamilton turned to Major Barrie who reluctantly left the room.

"I have seen you before Mr Hamilton in Berlin. You remember the Olympics in '36, you lunched at my house."

Hamilton looked confused.

"I do not know whether you recognize me, sir. I am Rudolf Hess. I am here on a mission of peace. The Führer does not want to defeat England. He is offering to stop the fighting."

"I am afraid I don't quite understand."

"I am on a mission of humanity, sir. My friend Albrecht Haushofer told me you were an Englishman who would understand our point of view. I wanted to meet you in Lisbon but we never got word."

"Hitler chose war when we wanted peace, Herr Hess. Now he wants peace and we have chosen war. I am curious about your flight. So you flew from Augsburg?"

"Yes, I left Augsburg at 5 o'clock."

"I have seen your map with your flight plan. Why did you fly east and then north when you hit the Dutch coast?"

Hess's face lit up as Hamilton pulled out the map that Major Barrie had taken away.

"The aim was to avoid British radar, Mr Hamilton."

"You flew several times back and forth here at the top of the rectangle. Why not head directly for your destination? You lost an hour of air time. Why?"

"My idea was to arrive after dark in Scotland, but I miscalculated the arrival time. It was still light when I came over land at 10 o'clock. So once in the air, I had to delay my arrival time."

In the early morning light Wing Commander Hamilton and MI6 Major Frank Foley visit the crash site of Hess' Messerschmitt airplane accompanied by several RAF officers. There were parts of the Me110 scattered across the field. They focussed their attention on the main fuselage section showing the markings NJ+OQ. Two officers arrived with the twisted remains of the aircraft guns.

"Look at this, sir," a young RAF officer said. "The guns are still packed in grease."

Foley and Hamilton looked at the guns astonished.

"This must be a training plane, perhaps?" Foley asked. "What do you think, Commander?"

"Obviously, he never intended to defend himself from our fighters," Hamilton replied.

"The plane could have been in storage, sir," the RAF officer said. "Maybe they didn't have time to prepare the guns for the flight."

"Yes, a plane that wasn't required, sitting idle somewhere," Foley said looking unconvinced. "I doubt there are many Me110s sitting idle with their bombing campaign going on. They need every plane they've got."

"I wonder where he came from," Hamilton said. "The Me110 is a short range aircraft without auxiliary tanks."

"What is the range on the Me110?" Foley asked.

"About 850 miles. There is no way a Me110 could make it

this far north without refuelling."

"You said he lost a lot of time in the air flying back and forth in that box over the North Sea. So if he didn't refuel, he must have flown in from somewhere closer. Denmark? Norway?"

Hamilton nodded in agreement.

"He wouldn't have sufficient petrol to fly directly from Augsburg. That's easily 1,000 miles, perhaps more with lost time, unless, of course, he had drop tanks."

"You think he had drop tanks?" Foley asked.

"He certainly wasn't trying to save fuel coming in as fast as he did. When we lost him, he was flying at more than 300 mph. No pilot would do that with an almost empty fuel tank."

An RAF officer called them over to look at a wing section.

"You can still smell the petrol, sir. It looks like he still had several gallons left in the tank when he crashed the plane."

Foley and Hamilton looked at each other mystified.

In the infirmary a young army doctor examined Hess' wrenched ankle, moving it around to check for mobility. After a moment Dr Graham looked up at Hess.

"*Keine Fraktur.* I don't think it is broken, sir."

"*Gut.*"

"Maybe you pulled a tendon or a muscle. You should not be walking on it for a while."

Graham bound Hess' ankle tightly with a cotton wrap.

"This should help immobilize the ankle."

"I need to talk to Mr Hamilton again, sir. Can you tell him? I need him to send a telegram to inform my family that I am in good health."

Graham finished attaching the wrap, but remained silent.

"Please, *Herr Doktor.*"

"You better take that up with Major Barrie, sir. I can't help you. "

Eight

At the RAF Northolt airfield near London, Commander Hamilton climbed out of a Hurricane fighter and walked towards a waiting car on the tarmac with a small bag. The driver stepped out and opened the back door for the commander. The car drove away silently into the failing light.

It was dark by the time Hamilton's car arrived at Ditchley Park, a magnificent country house near Charlbury in Oxfordshire. The car stopped at the gate manned by two soldiers before being allowed to approach the house. At the front entrance, a very tired Hamilton climbed out of the car and headed for the entrance. A servant opened the door for the new arrival and led him up the stairs to the second-floor dining room.

"Please wait here, sir."

The servant showed Hamilton into the library with its leather chairs and floor-to-ceiling bookcases before disappearing down the stairs.

Inside the dining room, the distinguished guests were finishing up their evening meal in the baroque hall. The oil paintings of illustrious family members looked down on the dinner guests, lit by the reddish glow from the fireplace. The windows were blacked out with heavy drapes for security reasons.

Among the guests, Prime Minister Winston Churchill sat at the head of the table drinking brandy, puffing on a cigar and conversing with members of his cabinet in their home away from home - one of their many weekend jaunts to avoid the German bombings in London.

Just as the dinner party was breaking up, Commander Hamilton was ushered into the room by a military attaché. The Air Minister Archibald Sinclair stood up to greet him.

"Please join us, Douglas. You must be exhausted."

Reading a dispatch, Churchill turned briefly toward Hamilton in a jovial mood and shook his hand.

"A glass of pinot noir, perhaps or maybe a whisky for Commander Hamilton?"

"Wine will be fine, sir."

A waiter approached with a clean glass and poured Hamilton a glass of red.

"So what is this funny story of yours, Commander?" Churchill asked.

"The German airman says he is Rudolf Hess, the deputy *Reichsminister*, and he looks the part."

Hamilton passed a small photograph to Churchill, who looked at a picture of Hess with his son at their summer house in Bavaria.

'Well, well."

"He had no identity cards with him, just some family snaps and an envelope addressed to Hauptmann Alfred Horn. He says he's on a peace mission, sir."

"This is quite preposterous," Churchill said. "The deputy *Reichsminister*. Hitler's right-hand man in Scotland. A Nazi Beelzebub rising over the dales."

Sinclair suppressed a laugh.

"Douglas, you realize just how ridiculous all this sounds," Sinclair said.

"I know, sir."

"Hess was in Landsberg Prison with Hitler. He contributed to that dreadful book, *Mein Kampf.* I think it was Hess who introduced the notion of *Lebensraum* from that fellow Karl Haushofer," Churchill said.

A butler knocked on the door. Churchill stood up and took a puff on his cigar.

"Time for a bit of entertainment, Archie. Hess or no Hess. I'm going to see the Marx brothers. Don't go away, young man. We'll talk later."

"Yes, sir."

Hamilton watched as Churchill and his cabinet left the room, followed by senior staff, many carrying their drinks. Sinclair hung back with Hamilton.

"The PM likes a bit of relaxation after a meal. Are you sure you are alright, Douglas?"

Hamilton picked up his wine glass and rubbed the sleep from his eyes.

"You look knackered. Let me find you a room. You might want to take a nap. It will be a long night."

In the dark infirmary, Hess awakened to a cold draught from the window. He was dressed in grey flannel pyjamas and covered by a brown army blanket. He tried to return to sleep but was kept awake by a gruff voice in German addressing him through the open door.

"*Ihr Name, bitte?* Your name, please?"

"*Herr Oberst.* I am Rudolf Hess."

"Date of birth?"

"Born in 1894."

"Place of birth?"

"Alexandria, Egypt."

"Are you ready for war, soldier?"

Hess sat up, tucked in his belly, and saluted his superior officer in the shadows.

"I am ready."

"*Sehr gut. Heil, Hitler.*"

The voice of Herr Oberst faded away and Hess reclined in his bed, returning to a deep sleep.

Nine

A soldier stumbled into the moonlit infirmary with two visitors in the early morning hours.

"Got some visitors to see you, Mr Horn," the soldier said in a loud voice as he banged on the door.

Hess woke up with a start, shielded his eyes from the sudden glare of light from a naked light bulb. Two men were standing in the doorway to the infirmary. Hess quickly sat up in bed rubbing his eyes.

"Sorry to disturb you at such a late hour," Commander Hamilton said. "I would like you to meet Mr Ivone Kirkpatrick, who has come from London to see you."

"I'll leave you to it then, Mr Horn," the soldier said as he disappeared out the door leaving the visitors to dust off the chairs and make themselves comfortable.

Hess looked long and hard at Kirkpatrick, an elegant gentleman with a neat moustache who had been the First Secretary at the British Embassy in Berlin from 1933 to 1938.

"What time is it?" Hess asked.

"Very late or very early depending on your taste for these things," Hamilton said.

"I think it is very early," Hess said now wide awake. "The day is new."

Hess grabbed several pages of handwritten notes and swung his legs off the bed.

"I think I have seen you before, perhaps in Berlin in '36. Do you remember me?"

Kirkpatrick nodded as Hess looked at his notes.

"As I mentioned to Commander Hamilton, I am here on a mission of peace. I was sent by the Führer who seeks a peace settlement with Britain. I am the Deputy *Reichsminister* so I am in a position to negotiate the terms of the peace. German forces will reduce all of Britain to rubble if Britain doesn't accept the peace settlement. You have no chance of winning this war against superior German forces."

Kirkpatrick was curious to know more about Hess and his plans for peace while Hamilton's interest was already waning.

"Will Hitler invade England?" Kirkpatrick asked.

"No one can know for sure. I am his closest confidant and I speak with complete authority, but I cannot know this. I can give you my word that the Führer has never entertained any designs against the British empire."

Outside the Maryhill Barracks, the dawn light was coming up in the east as the two men emerged from the building after three hours of listening to Hess' tedious monologue on Anglo-German relations. In the car park, headlights came on and a black Hillman advanced slowly to collect the men on the front steps.

Kirkpatrick turned to Hamilton.

"I will call the Foreign Secretary from Edinburgh."

"What was all that claptrap about?"

"Bloody Hun nonsense," said Kirkpatrick.

"You believe him? Do you think he is Hess?"

"I think there is little doubt to his identity. A German radio broadcast announced earlier this evening that Hess was missing. Who else can he be?"

"I know he looks like Hess, but after meeting him twice, I am not so sure."

The car pulled up and the two men got in.

A cortege composed of a black Lincoln, an unmarked ambulance, and an old Wolseley sedan drove through the rubble of London's streets. A pall of smoke hung over the city after the recent German bombing.

As Hess was flying over the hedgerows in Scotland, London was attacked by 550 German bombers, wrecking a large part of the city. The chamber of the House of Commons was destroyed and parts of Westminister Abbey were burned. Some 3,000 people were killed or wounded.

The cortege drove through the gates of the Tower of London and stopped at a guardhouse. Hess disembarked in a courtyard dating back to the Middle Ages where many perfectly innocent men and women were sent to their death over the centuries. He was led into an old building, now converted into a prison, by two men in trench coats, under the watchful eye of the Yeomen Warders carrying Sten submachine guns in their black and red uniforms and hats.

Ten

Berlin 1973

"London was in ruins after the worst bombing of the war and this man Hess was proposing a peace treaty with Hitler, which would compromise the PM's plan to bring the Americans into the war," Cummings said. "The timing was terrible."

A waiter arrived with a beer for Dr Terry.

"Peace was not in the cards for Churchill, who was running a war on several continents with little or no success," Cummings continued. "Two days after the bombing of London, the RAF bombed Hamburg, Emden and Berlin in retaliation."

"What did the Germans have to say about Hess?" Terry asked, sipping his beer.

"The Germans had announced that Hess was a victim of hallucinations and mental derangement. They were clearly washing their hands of him. Meanwhile, Churchill had Hess put in the tower so the intelligence services could have a go at him."

NICHOLAS KINSEY

London, May 1941

In the interrogation room at Latchmere House, MI6 Major Frank Foley and Captain Short sat at a table with the chief interrogator, Lt-Colonel Robin 'Tin Eye' Stephens in his Gurkha uniform and monocle.

Hess in his Luftwaffe uniform was brought in, limping on his right leg by two soldiers. The men at the table ignored the prisoner as Stephens consulted his file and prepared his questions.

Stephens was an expert interrogator born in Egypt and educated at a Lycée Francais, before spending years as an officer among the Gurkhas, the elite regiment of Nepalese troops in the British army. He spoke seven languages, including Urdu, Arabic, Somali, French and, of course, German. He was xenophobic, hated homosexuals and Germans alike, and had a record of breaking down even the most hardened of spies.

Behind his round spectacles and mild manner, Major Foley was an astute intellectual with a penetrating gaze. He was a defrocked priest who later became a passport control officer in Berlin during the 1930s. He bent the rules and helped thousands of Jewish families without papers escape from Nazi Germany. He had been invited by Stephens to assist with the interrogation in a passive role but had been warned in strong language not to utter a single word.

Stephens was a stickler for the rules and didn't condone violence of any kind. The prisoners were to be brought in one at a time and no two prisoners were to be seen walking in the hallways. Prisoners were often hooded for long periods and deprived of sleep. The silence at Latchmere was maintained even by the guards who wore tennis shoes to keep down the noise.

"Can I have a chair, sir? My ankle is hurting," Hess complained, looking at the three men behind the table, hoping for a bit of empathy.

"A chair, please?"

Stephens glared at Hess.

"Hauptmann Horn, you are in a British Secret Service prison at the present time. You are a prisoner of war. You will remain standing. It is our job to determine who you are, be it Hauptmann Horn, Rudolf Hess, or just some bad actor. *Verstehen Sie?*"

The silence continued. An officer came in and handed a piece of paper to Stephens, who looked at it and then put it in the file. Stephens sorted the papers and then closed the file.

"*Wo sind Ihre Papiere?* Where are your papers?"

"I lost them, sir."

"*Keinen Ausweis, Herr Horn*? You have no identity card, no party membership card, no passport. All you have is an envelope with your name on it. Are you a member of the party?"

"Of course."

"Well, if you pretend to be the Deputy *Reichsminister*, you should remember his card number?"

"I forget," Hess replied nervously.

"I thought Hess was an early member of the party?"

"Yes, sir."

"Then it should be easy to remember. Could it be number 24 or maybe number 16?"

Hess looked truly stumped by the question as he scratched his head.

"I am not sure, sir."

Stephens looked down at his notes.

"Wo sind Sie geboren, Herr Horn? Where were you born?"
"Ich bin Rudolf Hess. Mein Name ist Rudolf Hess ."
"Place of birth?"
"Alexandria, Egypt."

Near the observation window, Agent Paul Cummings was fascinated by the appearance of the prisoner whose resemblance to the *Reichsminister* was remarkable. In contrast to the pictures of Rudolf Hess in the newsreels, this man was very thin. He was gaunt, hollow-cheeked, and pale with a receding forehead, thick bushy eyebrows, deeply sunken eyes and irregular teeth. If this was the real Rudolf Hess, Cummings wondered what had happened to the man since he was last seen on the big screen and in the newspapers.

Near Cummings sat a stenographer doing a transcript of the testimony on her machine. He smiled at the stenographer, who looked up briefly to acknowledge him, but continued her work at a furious pace.

Cummings was reading a top secret file on Hess as an attractive dark-haired woman in a WAAC (Women's Auxiliary Army Corp) uniform entered the room and approached the observation window. Claudia put her hand on her husband's arm and froze at the sight of the prisoner.

"Dieser Mann ist nicht Hess, Paul. This man is not Hess."

"I don't know, Claudia."

"Hess is not so thin, Paul. Look at his eyes, he has been deprived of food. He can't be Hess, the *Reichsminister."*

"He could have lost weight, Claudia. He certainly looks like the man. Maybe he has been in prison?"

Claudia looked at her husband, clearly unconvinced. She was Jewish with jet black hair, small regular features and green eyes. It was her laugh, which was her best feature, when her whole face lit up with liveliness and joy. Her thoughts returned to her life as a Jewish refugee in Cologne before the war, and she instantly felt fear and consternation at the sight of the Nazi in the next room.

In the interrogation room, Stephens continued with his questions.

"Your parents' first names?"

"Fritz and Klara, sir."

"Any brothers or sisters?"

"Alfred is my younger brother. I have a sister."

"Name, bitte. Name, please."

"Margarete."

Stephens consulted his file.

"Your date of birth?"

"April 26, 1896."

"Your age?"

"47, sir."

"You mean 45, don't you? Perhaps the date of birth is erroneous. What do you say?"

Hess looked perplexed. He remained silent, looking down at the floor.

"Where did you live in Alexandria? What street?"

"Die Straße? Ich kann mich nicht erinnern. I don't remember. My father had a big house in Ibrahimieh."

"Do you remember your school in Ibrahimieh? What was the name?"

"That was a long time ago. I can't remember."

Hess laughed nervously.

"Well, do you remember your teachers?"

"Not very well."

"What do you remember from Egypt?"

"The house, my mother."

"Do you remember the beach? There is a famous restaurant on the beach."

"No. I am tired, sir. How long will this go on?"

Stephens looked down at the file on the table. Short passed him a document, which he looked at briefly.

"We are simply having a conversation, Mr Horn. I ask a question and you answer to the best of your abilities. German agents who lie to us are hanged."

"Yes, sir."

"Let's move on. After your time in Egypt, your family returned to Germany. Where did you go for your schooling?"

"*Evangelisches Pädagogium im Bad-Godesberg.*"

"It's on the river, isn't it?"

Hess nodded.

"Bad Godesberg is on the Main or is it the Neckar?"

"I don't remember."

"You don't remember? Of course, you do. I think it is neither. It's on the Rhine."

Hess knew he was doing badly and was fearful of the consequences if he didn't satisfy his interrogators. But this monocled Prussian fellow, like some stereotypical Teutonic knight, was slowly driving him mad with his questions.

"You must remember the school in Bad Godesberg. It's a pretty place. You have a famous colleague from the same school. Do you know his name?"

"I am very tired, sir. Will this continue for long?"

"I will give you a hint. *Deutsche Arbeitsfront.* The German Labour Front."

"DAF? I am sorry I don't know this man."

"Come on, Horn. He is quite famous in Germany. They even named a ship after him. You know the KdF, *Kraft durch Freude*. Strength through joy and all that malarkey."

Hess' thoughts went to the KdF, which was a large state-operated leisure organization in Nazi Germany, and was part of the DAF. It was set up to promote the social values of National Socialism and became a large tourism operator. It rewarded workers with concerts, plays, library visits, day trips and holidays.

"Yes, of course, I know. The Führer was behind the KdF."

"Last chance, Horn. Name of your colleague?"

"I am tired, sir. I can't remember."

"Robert Ley. You went to the same school as *Herr Ley*. He is a little older than you. You went to the same meetings. He is well known and close to Hitler, I think."

"No, he is not. I am close to Hitler. That is why he sent me here with a peace plan."

As Stephens opened his file and searched for a picture, Foley stood up and left the room.

In the observation room, Cummings and his wife were fascinated by the interrogation.

"Tin Eye has done it again," Cummings said.

"What a ridiculous man to come here posing as Rudolf Hess," Claudia replied.

The woman stenographer told them to keep their voices down as Major Foley entered the room.

"Stephens is doing a wonderful job. You know he was born in Egypt, knows the place like the back of his hand."

Cummings nodded his agreement.

"Nothing gets by him."

"Hess became a member of the party in 1920," Claudia said. "His number is 16, an easy number to remember."

"Good point," Foley said. "I am sure Hess would be very proud of the fact that he was an early member of the party."

"What about the date of birth?" Cummings asked.

"I think Rudolf Hess is actually 47, so the date of birth must be wrong. He told the doctor in Scotland that he had two sisters. He complains of memory lapses."

"So what does MI6 want from us, Major?" Cummings asked.

"'C' wants the whole background. He wants to know where this man comes from, who trained him, the when, the where, and the how. He knows things that could be useful to us. I doubt we are going to get a confession the hard way."

"We have the people, but it will take time," Cummings said, looking at Claudia.

"You have the time. He isn't going anywhere."

"Do you have a place where we can start work, Major?"

"Not yet. We are looking for a safe house. There may be a threat to his life, so we need to protect him."

Foley paused as he looked at Cummings and his wife. Cummings was a Foley recruit, and they had worked together in Berlin before the war. He knew that Cummings would get to the heart of the matter in record time. He was a clever officer with a natural ability to read people and situations, and his German was excellent. And, of course, it didn't hurt to have an attractive Jewish wife with similar skills working for him.

"Hess is a prisoner of war and is to have special treatment, orders from the PM's office," Foley said. "You will have to take very good care of him."

"Don't worry, sir. We will."

Eleven

In a South London row house, Paul Cummings stepped into the tiny living room where a small child Steffi - three years old - played on the floor. Claudia entered from the kitchen in her WAAC uniform.

"I just got in. Mama called. They are going to adopt Veronika."

"That's wonderful news. How old is she now?"

"Nine. It's been almost a year since she arrived in Harwich with the *Kindertransport* kids."

Cummings removed his coat and went to the drinks table. He poured himself a whisky and sat down, watching Steffi on the floor while Claudia prepared the evening meal in the kitchen. He remembered the day that Claudia and her parents, Markus and Rosa, left Cologne on the boat train with their British visas.

Cologne 1937

At the railway station, numerous families were waiting in line for the arrival of the Jewish Relief Organization with their emigration papers. The German police had herded the Jews into a long line along the platform and wouldn't allow them onto the train without travel documents.

Claudia Heller and her parents waited in the line with their bags while her cousin Anna, husband Geert and young Veronika stood nearby to see them off. The young British passport officer Paul Cummings arrived and went up to the police officer in front of the line.

"Ich habe die Ausweise für Großbritannien. I have the passes for Great Britain."

"Bitte, geben Sie mir die Namen. Give me the names."

The policeman took the list and started calling the names: "Ackerfeld, *zwei Personen.* Bernstein. Dressler, *drei Personen.* Ehrlich. Fertig, *zwei Personen.* Heller, *drei Personen...*"

As the families exited the line, Cummings handed them their temporary immigration visas for Britain. Claudia Heller arrived with her parents, each carrying a single suitcase. In that fleeting moment, as Cummings handed Claudia the visas, she took his hand in hers and squeezed it.

"Ich bin in dich verliebt. I love you," she whispered, "see you in London."

"Vielen Dank, Paul. Thank you so much," said Markus and Rosa.

Cummings tried to maintain his professional composure as Claudia and her parents hurried away towards the train, followed by their friends Anna and Geert with young Veronika in tow.

A whistle was blown. From their compartment, Claudia, Markus and Rosa waved at their friends as the train started to move out of the station. Claudia blew kisses at young Cummings standing on the platform among the crowd. He waved at Claudia and noticed young Veronika smiling at him while her parents, Anna and Geert, watched with a sense of foreboding as the train left the station.

London 1941

Cummings felt a wistful longing for the past as he recalled young Veronika's smiling face at the train station. Claudia called to him from the kitchen.

"Her parents, Anna and Geert, are still in Dachau, you know. Mama has had no news from them for quite some time."

"Anna is your second cousin? So that would make Veronika a second cousin once removed?"

"Yes, I don't know her well. Her husband Geert was arrested for stealing artwork from his own gallery, a ridiculous charge. Then they came for Anna, who managed to hide Veronika with the neighbours. That's all I know."

"Well, Veronika is lucky to be here at all, catching the last ship out of Amsterdam," Cummings said.

Claudia, wearing an apron, stepped into the living room.

"Mama wants us to come down to celebrate. This is a big moment for her and papa."

"Well, that is wonderful news. I am not sure we can get away. I talked to Major Foley again. Hess is sticking to his story, so the major wants us to move out to Mytchett in Surrey next week. It's about 35 miles from here, off in the country. They are looking for a house for us. What do you think?"

Claudia emitted a high-pitched whoop and rushed to embrace her husband.

"That's wonderful. It will give us a break from the city."

Young Steffi jumped up from the floor with a cry and ran to hug her parents. Cummings collected Steffi in his arms.

"With the warm weather, Steffi will be able to play outside.

Won't you, *Schatzi*?" Claudia said.

"Do you remember Bayreuth, Horn?" Lt-Colonel Stephens asked Hess several days later at Latchmere House in the company of Captain Short.

Hess had been held in complete isolation for several days. He stood in the middle of the room in clean clothes and appeared less distracted by the pain in his leg.

"Bayreuth?" Hess asked.

"Don't you like the music of Wagner?"

"Of course, he is a great German composer."

"Your boss likes his Wagner. *Der Ring des Niebelungen? Die Walküre?* How about you?"

"Yes, every German likes Wagner."

"Hitler adores Wagner, is what I hear. He goes every summer to Bayreuth. You ever go with him?"

"I am not sure."

"Maybe you remember the name of the hotel?"

"I want to stop. I don't like games."

"Mr Horn, we are not playing games here. I am simply asking you the necessary questions to establish your identity. Does Hotel Bube mean anything to you, Mr Horn?"

Hess looked at Stephens with a blank expression.

"You are a public figure and you travel with the most photographed man in history. Take a look at this picture of you and the Führer together."

Hess approached the table to look at the picture of Hitler and Hess leaving the Hotel Bube in Bayreuth among a crowd of Nazi supporters. Hess shrugged his shoulders indifferently.

"I cannot remember everything I did with the Führer."

Stephens put the photograph back in the file and glanced at

another document.

"Tell me about your parent's house in Reicholdsgrün."

"It is in Bavaria, sir. We spent our summers there."

"What is the nearest town?"

"It is a small place, sir."

"You remember the town of Wunsiedel? It is nearby. Tell me about your summers there."

Hess said nothing.

"Did you swim in the lakes? Visit Wunsiedel?"

"Of course, it is a beautiful place."

"Did you visit the caves?"

"Caves? There are no caves."

"You don't remember the Luisenberg caves. You must have gone with your family?"

Hess looked down at his hands just as the lights went out and the room was plunged into darkness. A siren sounded somewhere within the Latchmere complex. A soldier stepped into the interrogation room, dimly lit by the bluish light from a blacked-out window.

"Sir, we have an emergency."

Stephens and Short seized Hess and rushed him out of the room, leaving their files behind. Short pulled out his Webley revolver as they moved into the hall and approached the staircase with a terrified Hess. The soldier illuminated the way with a torch, moving ahead of the group as they descended the stairs to the lower landing. Gunshots were heard coming from below. Stephens grabbed Hess by the scruff of the neck and held him back as Short and the soldier ran on ahead. Shouts and running feet were heard throughout the building as complete chaos invaded the interrogation centre.

Twelve

Mytchett 1941

A black Lincoln followed by an ambulance and a Wolseley sedan entered Camp Z in Surrey, near Farnborough. The camp was a fortified military installation with a guardhouse and machine gun pits on the perimeter. In the middle of the estate was Mytchett house, a run-down Victorian red-brick mansion, surrounded by gardens with a view of a small lake.

Scots Guards in typical Glengarry caps with the red and white dicing and red toories on top carried Lee Enfields and Bren light machine guns. The garden was encircled by barbed wire and patrolled by Coldstream Guards.

The ambulance pulled up at the front door, and Hess stepped out, accompanied by two Scots Guards. They brought him upstairs to a large room on the second floor with a steel mesh grille covering the central window. In the corner, there was a WC with a cold water tap and sink. Along the wall near the window, a table with neatly piled books in German and English overlooked the garden and the machine gun pits.

Lt Malone, who hailed from the Canadian prairies, put Hess' gunny sack with his clothes on the table as the prisoner sat on the bed exhausted. Lt Jackson went to the window to air the room.

"Everything alright, sir?" Malone asked.

Hess remained silent.

"Your dinner will be served soon," Jackson added.

After the young men had left the room, Hess stood up and went to the window looking out on the garden. Several armed men patrolled the perimeter.

Hess went to the door, which had been left open, and stepped out onto the landing. He looked right toward the guardroom on the same floor where Malone and Jackson shared a room. He looked left towards the metal gate barring access to the stairs, where a guard observed him from the other side.

As the dawn light came up, a military staff car drove into the grounds of Camp Z. Major Foley and Agent Cummings disembarked and entered Mytchett House, showing their passes to a Scots Guards officer.

Dr Dicks still in his dressing gown, stepped into the small downstairs office, followed by Foley and Cummings. They pulled some mismatched chairs together around a large desk and sat down. A kitchen staffer in a white apron brought tea for the men.

"Sorry for this impromptu visit, Doctor," Foley said. "This is Paul Cummings, who will be working with you."

Cummings shook hands with the doctor.

"Dr Dicks is a psychiatrist in the Army Medical Corp. He's worked with our services on several occasions."

Dicks poured the tea for his guests.

"I heard the chaps over at Latchmere had a bit of a scare yesterday, Major."

Foley frowned at this remark, realizing that gossip about the top secret facility was already making the rounds.

"A German agent pulled a gun off one of our guards during a blackout and tried to shoot his way out of Latchmere," Foley said. "He shot young Farnsworth. The poor chap's condition is still critical. We hope he pulls through."

"Did the agent escape?" Cummings asked.

"The guards tackled him in the nick of time. Luckily, only Farnsworth was injured."

Foley turned to Dicks.

"The reason for the meeting this morning is to set up the procedures for handling the prisoner. The instructions from the PM's office are to treat him as a very special prisoner of war. He is potentially a war criminal, but he should be treated with the same respect as an important German officer."

Foley read from his notes.

"He will have food, books, writing materials and limited recreation. He is not to have access to newspapers or radio. He shall have no contact with the outer world and no visitors are allowed without Foreign Office approval. That's about it, gentlemen."

Foley put away his notes.

"Concerning the name of the prisoner, our orders are to refer to him as 'Z' at all times as in 'Camp Z', the name of this facility. We are to avoid using the name Hess or Horn, unless we are talking to him directly."

"That's fine, sir," Dicks said.

Foley turned to Cummings.

"Our non-official aim, of course, is to prise out of the man as many secrets as we can about the Nazi leadership. Dr Dicks will assist us by monitoring the prisoner's health on a daily basis and glean a maximum amount of information."

Foley paused to drink his tea.

"How is the prisoner this morning?" Foley asked.

"He isn't up yet, Major," Dicks replied. "Lt Malone and Lt Jackson have a room on the same floor."

"What's your impression of Malone and Jackson, Doctor?" Cummings asked.

"Very likeable, both of them. Nice, well-behaved young men. Malone is a Canadian and a very nice chap."

"Very good. I have prepared a list of my people who will be arriving shortly."

Cummings handed the list to the major.

"I will set it up with the commanding officer," Foley replied. "There shouldn't be any problems."

"We'll do our best, Major," Dicks said. "We'll treat him well."

Foley nodded, turning to Cummings. "I hope your family is comfortable in the new accommodations, Paul. We scrambled to put it together on short notice."

"Claudia loves it, particularly the garden. It is a bit run down with the leaky roof, but we will manage. The change from London will do us good."

In the prisoner's room, Z in his newly requisitioned pyjamas stared at a glass of water on the table as sunlight crept into the room through the blackout curtains. He picked up the glass and peered at the water through his banged-up spectacles.

He went to the window and looked down at the sentries patrolling the garden through the drapes and then turned his attention to the steel grille running his fingers over the bars. He flipped casually through the books on the table and then walked around the room, looking at the walls. He stopped at the door, noticing that there was no way to open it from the inside because the handle had been removed. He looked up to see a small loudspeaker on the wall.

Hearing footsteps on the stairs, he stepped back just as the door opened and Lt Malone entered the room.

"Morning, sir. What would you like for breakfast? I will bring it up on a tray."

Malone busied himself at the window, pulling the drapes while he waited for a reply. Z sat on the bed watching the lieutenant.

"Tea, bread, bacon, fish, if you have it."

"Of course, sir. Fish is not rationed, but bacon, cheese, and butter are. I saw eggs are going to be rationed starting next week."

"This is quite a hardship, I think."

"Don't worry, sir. There is no rationing here at Mytchett House. You are in His Majesty's service. We eat very well."

Malone headed for the door.

Z washed his hands and face at the small sink with cold water from the tap in the tiny WC. He looked around and grabbed a towel from a shelf, wiping his face and hands. He looked for a mirror, but there was none. He looked up and noticed another loudspeaker fixed to the ceiling. From the other room, he heard Malone's voice calling to him.

"It's on the table, sir."

Z stuck his head out of the WC and nodded to Malone.

"I heard the siren last night, Lieutenant."

"False alarm, sir."

"These sirens come on every night?"

"No, sir. They're mainly for the rare emergency: air raids or breaches in security."

"Air raids?"

"Few this far west, sir. Your friends in the Luftwaffe prefer to bomb central London."

Z noted the sarcasm but said nothing.

"I would like to make a few German desserts for the prisoner. What do you think, Betty?" Claudia asked the cook.

"I don't know nothin' about German food, love. Maybe Hilda here can help you with the preparation."

Claudia was in the kitchen getting to know the staff. Betty was a large round woman with red cheeks while her helper, Hilda, was a slim wisp of a girl with freckles.

"Well, don't worry," Claudia said. "I can always make them myself."

"You give me the recipe and I can do 'em for you, miss," Hilda said, stepping forward as Betty removed a tray of biscuits from the oven.

"Thank you, Hilda."

Hilda started to remove the biscuits from the tray as Betty poured chicken broth into a saucepan. The women looked up as Captain Cummings in his new Scots Guards uniform entered the kitchen and approached Claudia.

"Hello, ladies. I'm Captain Cummings. So Claudia, what are your plans for food for the prisoner?"

"I think that Z may have a sweet tooth for German desserts like *Apfelstrudel, Marmorkuchen, Windbeutel, Rumkugeln* (apple strudel, marble cake, cream puffs, rum chocolate balls). That kind of thing."

A short wiry man with red curly hair, Werner came up the stairs from the basement and joined them.

"Morning, Claudia. Betty, Hilda, morning ladies. Good idea, *Rumkugeln*, Claudia. I think you will need my help in the kitchen."

Claudia laughed as she put a tea set on a tray and headed for the dining area, followed by Cummings and Werner. They sat down for their meeting in the empty room.

"That might be a good idea, Werner," Cummings said. "You need to be visible in the kitchen from time to time helping out."

"Right, sir," Werner replied.

"Z needs to see both of you working in the kitchen."

Claudia poured the tea.

"Werner and I have discussed our cover, Paul," Claudia said. "We could be German kitchen staff on loan from Trent Park. Their Luftwaffe pilots and U-boat officers get German cuisine, schnapps and whisky, and walks in the park. The very best treatment."

"I hear they are a talkative bunch," Werner said. "A lot of bored officers with nothing to do but eat and drink."

"Trent Park is starting to produce results from what I have heard," Cummings said. "So it is reasonable to suppose that Z would get the same. Excellent idea, Claudia. I think it will only work if you and Werner dumb down a bit. You need more of the sweaty *Hausfrau* look."

"Am I too elegant for you, Captain Cummings?" Claudia joked.

Cummings smiled at his wife.

"I can do that, sir," Werner said. "A limp, an unshaven look, dirty clothes."

"We'll go with it. I think you both know what I mean. When is Martin coming in?"

"Tomorrow, sir," Werner said.

"With Z cut off from the news, we may want to use the occasional German radio broadcast to provoke a reaction from him. Can you set it up?"

"Yes, I can play the broadcasts back on my fake radio," Werner said. "I have the contact at the BBC."

Thirteen

Z was reading a book in German when he was interrupted by a knock on the door and the arrival of Cummings in his new uniform.

"Sir, I have come for the tray."

Z nodded at Cummings.

"I am Captain Cummings. I work with Lt Malone and Lt Jackson."

Cummings picked up the tray with the bacon, kipper and tea practically untouched.

"Are you sure you have finished, sir?"

Z signalled to Cummings to come closer and whispered in his ear.

"I don't trust Lt Malone, Captain. I think he is poisoning the food."

"I wouldn't know about that, sir. You might want to talk to Dr Dicks. Let me have a taste."

Cummings picked up the kipper and bit into it, washing it down with the tea while slurping loudly.

"Hard to say, sir. If you don't mind, I'll take the strips of bacon home with me for the children. Bacon is hard to find these days."

Cummings grabbed the tray and left.

PLAYING RUDOLF HESS

In the garden, the azaleas and tulips were in full bloom. Lt Malone and Lt Jackson went for a walk with the prisoner. They admired the fragrance of the hyacinths and primrose in the flower beds just coming into their own, but could not ignore the soldiers with their Bren submachine guns near a row of flowering dogwood trees.

"What a lovely garden," Z said.

"Not so lovely with the machine gun pits, sir," Malone replied.

Z looked at the soldiers watching them from behind their sandbagged gun emplacements.

"Yes," Z said mildly. "They have destroyed the view."

Jackson said: "It's unfortunate, sir, but it's for your own protection."

"My protection? Who would want to attack me?"

"I wouldn't know, sir," remarked Jackson.

Upstairs in the prisoner's quarters, Cummings slipped into Z's room. He checked the books on the table for hidden papers. He tossed the bed and then went into the WC, going down on all fours to examine possible hiding places. He stepped back into the larger room and looked closely at a famous Dürer woodcut print entitled *Melencolia* fixed to the common wall shared by the guards. In the print by the famous German renaissance master, an angel held its head in deep reflection as time ran out in an hourglass over its head.

Cummings went to the door and exited the room.

In the garden, Malone and Jackson returned from their walk

with the prisoner. Z looked tired and anxious.

Malone said: "Are you sure you are alright, sir?"

"I am fine, Lieutenant. I just need to lie down."

Z stumbled up the front steps.

"Tea is at five o'clock, sir," Malone said.

"Thank you."

Z climbed the stairs, followed by Malone and Jackson.

Back in his room, Z sat on his bed exhausted. He looked around the room and thought about his new English 'companions': Cummings, Malone, Jackson, and Doctor Dicks. Coming from Nazi Germany, he knew that these men were not simple soldiers, but obviously agents working for British secret services. With his knowledge of Gestapo techniques, he believed that as soon as he had been "squeezed dry" for intelligence purposes, he would be liquidated as a war criminal, probably in the guise of a suicide or by administering poison to his food.

He would have to remind his captors that he was a self-appointed German envoy and a Luftwaffe officer who had arrived openly in uniform and in an unarmed plane, and should be treated according to the Geneva Convention. Otherwise, his chances of remaining alive were slim. Surrounded by enemy agents, he would have to rely on his wits alone to survive.

It was a sunny afternoon as Captain Cummings arrived by the side door to the stable house and entered the backyard. The house was a one-storey dwelling with a walled garden. Claudia and Steffi sat in the yard in a wooden chair near some fruit trees and a vegetable patch invaded by weeds. Steffi spotted her father and ran towards him.

"There's your daddy," Claudia said. "You look very smart in your new uniform. How are you, *Liebling*?"

Cummings collected his daughter in his arms.

"I'm fine. You know I love it here, away from the city. It's so peaceful," Cummings said.

"Me, too. The air is clean, none of that London dust."

"Where's the sitter?"

"Lizzy just left. Her mum's not well, you know. Her brother Billy died in North Africa, and it has been a shock to the family."

"Yes, I believe she told me."

Cummings put down his briefcase and sat next to Claudia in the warm sunshine, cuddling Steffi in his arms.

"Paul, let's sit out here for a while and have a nice, strong drink. Supper can wait."

"It's lovely here."

"You know, I think Steffi misses her daddy," Claudia said as she watched the child sitting quietly on her dad's knee.

Fourteen

A gunshot boomed in the silence of the early morning followed by a siren. The Scots guards ran out to man their defensive positions as a huge spotlight lit up the sky. In his room, Z was awakened by the sound of the siren blasting out of the loudspeaker. He jumped out of bed, limping towards the window.

He pushed the blackout drapes aside to see soldiers running for the machine gun pits. He sat in a chair near the window, listening to the chaos in the garden and turned when he heard a gruff voice in the dark room.

"*Die Kameraden kommen, Soldat.* Comrades are coming."

"Comrades, Herr Oberst?"

"Do you have your rifle, soldier?"

"I am ready, Herr Oberst."

"*Die Kameraden kommen.*"

Herr Oberst's voice faded away, and Z's attention returned to the pandemonium in the garden.

"I heard you had a busy night," Captain Cummings said.

He was sitting in the downstairs office in conversation with Lt Malone, Lt Jackson and Dr Dicks.

"A full dress emergency, but it appears it was nothing. The men searched the perimeter, couldn't find any penetration of our defences," Dicks said.

"Two German parachutists were captured last week near the RAF interrogation centre at Cockfosters, so we need to be vigilant," Cummings said.

Malone and Jackson nodded in agreement.

"We need to keep our man in good health," Cummings said, "so you are to take him on walks and get him talking. It doesn't matter what you talk about. Talk about Germany before the war, about Hitler, about the Nazi party. It really doesn't matter. We need to be listening to the man if we want to monitor his mental health. You understand. This is important for Dr Dicks and for our mission here."

Cummings handed notebooks to the young men.

"I want you to keep a journal and take notes of your conversations with the man. Whatever he says, how he's feeling, anything. Write it down with the date and time immediately after the event."

"What do we do with our notes, Captain?" Malone said, flipping through his notebook and looking at the empty pages.

"Keep them with you. I will review them from time to time. The plan is to keep Z happy. I don't want to see any suicide attempts. We have had several German POWs kill themselves."

Dicks said: "I agree wholeheartedly with the captain, there will be hell to pay if this man kills himself."

"We will have him take his meals downstairs in a day or two," Cummings said. "I want you both to watch for stolen knives and forks. Any sharp instrument. It doesn't take much time to cut one's wrists or one's throat, for that matter."

Malone and Jackson nodded gravely.

"We will watch him, sir, do our best," Malone said.

"You know he fears being poisoned?" Cummings asked.

"But, sir, that's absurd. He eats the same food as we do," Jackson said.

"Remember, he is a POW, and it is quite common for prisoners to fear food poisoning," Dicks said.

Cummings nodded in agreement.

In the prisoner's room, Z looked out the window at the young men digging a new machine gun pit in the garden and then started writing a letter on A5 notepaper sitting at the table. He first wrote the date and then hesitated before continuing.

Den 5. Juni 1941

Sehr geehrter Herr Führer,

Ich habe für eine lange Zeit...

(June 5, 1941, Dear Leader, I have for a very long time...)

He stopped writing as Lt Malone entered the room with the food tray. He covered up the letter so Malone couldn't see it as he approached the table with the tray.

"Shepherd's pie, sir. I think you will like it. Betty's special."

Z looked at the meal hungrily as Malone left. He picked up the fork and started nibbling at the food. He turned it over in his mouth and swallowed slowly. He ate a bit more and then returned to his writing.

Z was visible at the table reading a book. The tray had been pushed away. He picked up his handwritten letter and slid it between several layers of tissue paper. He then rolled the letter tightly and slid it into the cracked spine of the old German book.

Through the spy hole in the guardroom, Captain Cummings watched Z's curious behaviour for a while longer as he flipped casually through several cheap novels from America belonging to Lt Malone. Detective novels with heroes such as Sam Spade, Philip Marlow, and The Spider. After a while, he put Malone's books down and glanced at Z one last time through the spy hole before walking down the hall to the prisoner's room and knocking on the door.

"Good day, sir. I've come for the tray."

Z remained silent, having barely touched the food.

"Is there something wrong with the food? Maybe Betty can cook up something special for you."

"I need to have a word with your superior, Captain."

"Well, sir. You can always talk to Dr Dicks. He's a good chap."

"Dr Dicks. He's the one who speaks good German?"

"Yes, sir."

"Where does the doctor come from?"

"I think he is Estonian, sir. He speaks German, Russian and French, I believe. A very nice man. You should talk to him if you have a problem."

Z awakened in the middle of the night to the sound of slamming doors and footsteps running up the stairs. There were voices and the rumbling sound of a motorcycle in the courtyard. Z pulled the pillow over his head as a voice from his past was heard, coming from the dark corner of the room.

"*Die Kameraden kommen, Soldat.*"

Z sat up suddenly.

"I admire your courage, soldier."

"I have courage, Herr Oberst. I am ready."

"*Die Kameraden kommen.* God be with us."

The voice of Herr Oberst faded away as Z waved his hands and whispered under his breath, fixing the shadows. He then stood up and went to the door, listening.

As he returned to bed, he noticed a very faint light source coming from the *Melencolia* woodcut fixed to the wall. The light was coming from the angel's eyes. He noticed that one of them was translucent and picking up light from the room next door. He stepped back, looking pensive.

Fifteen

The next day, the prisoner's door opened and Lt Malone stepped inside silently with the breakfast tray as Z struggled to wake up.

"Morning, sir."

Malone put the tray on the table.

"Got oatmeal this morning. I hope you like it."

Malone pulled the drapes from the windows, flooding the room with light. Z sat on the edge of his bed, looking exhausted. He regarded the lieutenant with suspicion as he left the room.

In the basement sound room, Captain Cummings sat down at a table with a pot of tea and teacups for the morning debriefing with his team. A small, bespectacled man, Martin was sitting at a nearby desk loaded with electronic eavesdropping equipment. He removed his headphones and came over to join them.

"Malone just brought in the breakfast tray," Martin said.

"Good. Anything else to report?"

"He talked again to this Herr Oberst, sir."

Cummings turned to Claudia.

"What do you think?"

"I think Herr Oberst may be Z's commanding officer. He fears him and has nightmares."

"What do you make of his remark about *'die Kameraden kommen'*?"

"I think it is wishful thinking, hoping his superior officer will come and save him."

Martin poured the tea.

"I don't think this Herr Oberst is real, sir," Martin said in his accented English. "Z is talking in his sleep. We can hear him tossing and turning in bed."

Werner picked up his cup of tea and said: "Maybe Herr Oberst is a father figure, sir? A childhood memory?"

"Well, this is a start. Thank you," Cummings said.

Claudia changed the subject.

"I have the *Apfelstrudel*, Paul. Perhaps you can take it up to him when you go in for the tray."

Captain Cummings led Z downstairs to the drawing room and knocked on the door.

"Come in," Dr Dicks said.

Cummings and Z entered the room to see Dicks sitting at the coffee table shuffling papers.

"Call me, Doctor, when you have finished. I will be outside the door."

"So Herr Hess, you have some complaints, I hear?"

Z sat down opposite the doctor and observed him for a moment.

"*Herr Doktor*, I promised the Führer that I would, under no circumstances, commit suicide. I have written a letter to him and warned him that news of my death might come from

Britain, but not to believe it. I think there are elements in Britain opposed to peace who might try to kill me."

"Try to kill you when you are well protected here with soldiers all around?" Dicks asked with a skeptical air.

"I fear it will come from the inside, a knife to the throat or through poison."

"Herr Hess, our orders are to treat you in the best possible manner. We have no intention of killing or poisoning you."

"As soon as I have no more value, Doctor. I will be liquidated as a war criminal. It is easy to do. I am surrounded by secret agents. They can put poison in my food or drive me to commit suicide."

"Really, Herr Hess. No one here would attempt to do such a thing, let me assure you."

As Dicks dismissed his concerns, Z fumed silently. He stood up and, without a word, headed for the door.

"Before you leave," Dicks said. "We have a request from the Foreign Office for a meeting on Thursday afternoon. It just arrived. I need to communicate your interest as soon as possible. Are you ready to meet with these people?"

Z's face lit up with the news, and his demeanour changed for the better.

"*Ja, Herr Doktor*. I am ready anytime."

"They are sending some very important people to meet with you. We can set up the meeting here in the drawing room if you like."

"That would be fine, sir. I will need to prepare myself."

"Prepare yourself?"

"For the meeting, sir."

The kitchen was quite primitive, with a cold water tap in a

white porcelain sink and drainboard, a large pantry near a coal-fired stove for cooking and heating during the winter months. Several buckets and paint cans were spread across the floor collecting rainwater from the leaky roof.

Young Lizzy was feeding Steffi at the kitchen table as Claudia climbed a stepladder and poked a hole through the roof with a broom handle.

"So you are German then, ma'am?" Lizzy asked.

"Yes, dear. I'm from Cologne. You know this damn roof is in a terrible state."

"The cottage ain't been lived in for a long while. So you be workin' with that husband of yours, the captain?"

"Yes, I am with the ATS - the Auxiliary Territorial Service. They were looking for German speakers. That's how I got the job."

"Whadda you do in Germany, ma'am?"

"Call me, Claudia. I was a music teacher before the war, Lizzy. I studied music. Can you hold this broom while I climb up on the roof?"

"You sure you wanna climb on the roof, ma'am?"

Lizzy looked astonished.

"Yes, dear. The roof leaks. Mr Evans gave me a few tiles to patch it up. We cannot live in a house with water dripping on the floor all the time."

Claudia handed the brush end of the broom to Lizzy to have her hold it in the hole.

"Keep your finger in the dike, Lizzy. I won't be long."

Claudia smiled at Steffi as she left the room carrying the stepladder, a new slate tile and a hammer. Once outside, she climbed the ladder and stepped onto the roof where the broom handle protruded from the broken tile. She peered through the hole at Lizzy and Steffi, standing on a kitchen chair.

"Hello, *Schatzi*. Can you see me?"

"Mummy, we see you," Steffi said, looking up at her mother with admiration.

"Of course you can. There are a few broken tiles that need to be replaced. Pull out the broom, Lizzy. I am going to put on a new tile."

Lizzy descended the broom as Claudia struck the broken tile with a hammer and slid the new one in place.

Sixteen

Cummings entered the prisoner's room to collect the tray. Z sat at the table looking at a book.

"Good day, sir. You don't like the food?"

"Lt Malone is trying to poison me, I know it."

"You don't like meat loaf?"

"I am the Führer's representative on a peace mission, Captain. I will not put up with this any longer. I need to be in the best possible health for a meeting with your government. Do you understand me?"

"But sir, the meat loaf is very good. It is the same I had for lunch and I am not sick."

"The meat loaf is very salty. This is to hide the poison."

Cummings tasted the food with a finger.

"You are right. It is a bit salty but surely not dangerous to eat."

Cummings pulled a piece of *Apfelstrudel* wrapped in cloth from his pocket.

"I have a surprise for you, sir."

"A surprise?"

"*E-i-n-e Ü-b-e-r-r-a-s-c-h-u-n-g*? That's my school German, sir. I still remember a bit."

Cummings laid the *Apfelstrudel* package on the table.

"We have a new cook, a German woman by the name of Claudia. She makes the cakes for the German officers over at Trent Park."

Z opened the package and held up the *Apfelstrudel*, looking at it closely. He nibbled on it slowly and then stuffed the rest into his mouth hungrily, watching Cummings, who smiled back at him.

"It is good, isn't it, sir?"

"*Sehr gut*, Captain."

Cummings nodded, collected the tray and left the room.

The downpour started just as Cummings arrived at the stable house. He ran for shelter into the kitchen, putting his briefcase on a chair. He put the kettle on the stove as the patter of heavy rain was heard coming from the roof.

"Claudia. I'm home."

He looked around and noticed that the usual buckets and paint cans for catching the rain had disappeared. He ran outside to grab a bucket from the porch and put it down on the kitchen floor watching for rain drops.

Claudia, in her ATS uniform, entered the room from the bedroom with young Steffi munching on a carrot lolly.

"Here's your daddy, *Schatzi*."

"Hello, darling. Oh, look at the carrot lolly," Cummings said, grinning at the child.

"I'd love a cup of tea, dear. I just got in," Claudia said.

"Coming up. The roof has stopped leaking. I don't know why."

"Did you repair it?" Claudia asked innocently.

"Well, no. I have been far too busy."

"Maybe it was Lizzy. I know Mr Evans came by with a few

replacement tiles."

"That girl wouldn't know how to repair a leaking roof in a million years," Cummings said.

"Well, it is quite a mystery," declared Claudia with an enigmatic smile.

"Yes, it is."

Cummings crossed to the stove to make the tea.

"We can go for a walk in the garden this afternoon, if you like, sir," Lt Malone said.

"Yes, I would like that, Lieutenant," Z replied.

They were sitting in the mess hall as Claudia in kitchen whites brought in hot soup on a tray for the new arrivals. Malone and Z sat at a table near Jackson and Cummings, listening to *Goodbye Sweetheart* by Al Bowlly on the radio. Across from them, the Scots Guards sneaked looks at the German prisoner.

Malone handed Z a bowl of soup from the tray and then took one for himself.

"I don't want this bowl, Lieutenant."

"Well, then have mine. I don't mind, sir."

Z took the bowl from Malone and started to gobble up the soup under the watchful eye of Cummings, who winked at Malone. The BBC news came on just as Z held up his bowl and poured the rest of the soup down the hatch. The Scots Guards smirked as they watched the prisoner's horrendous table manners.

The BBC announcer read:

"The latest news from the British fleet in the North Atlantic under Vice-Admiral Holland. The *HMS Hood, Norfolk,* and *Suffolk* intercepted the German battleship *Bismarck* and *Prinz*

Eugen off the coast of Greenland. The engagement began at 5:37 AM local time. During the action, the *HMS Hood* received an unlucky hit to a magazine and blew up. The explosion destroyed the aft part of the ship and the vessel sank in less than 3 minutes with no survivors. 1400 British servicemen have lost their lives."

The Scots Guards listened to the sad news as a young man named Ross suddenly stood up in shock, looking down at his friends.

The news report continued:

"The situation in Crete now appears hopeless and a full-scale retreat has been ordered. After the German parachutists suffered huge losses during their airborne invasion, they have now succeeded in taking the Maleme airfield and allied forces have been forced to retreat to the south coast. The situation remains tense."

In a state of shock, Ross murmured: "My brother John."

"What is it, Ross?" asked a colleague.

"My brother John is on the *Hood*."

George tried to comfort his friend as Z stood up, turning his soup bowl upside down, and gave a Nazi salute to the Scots Guards. He addressed Ross and his companions.

"You see, my friends, the British Navy will never sink the *Bismarck*. It is the greatest battleship ever built. It will destroy all your ships and our German U-boats will sink the rest. German forces have run you out of France, out of North Africa, out of the Balkans, Greece and Crete. You can go nowhere."

Cummings stepped quickly around the table as George and Ross reacted angrily to Z's insensitive outburst.

"That's a load of bollocks, you Nazi scum!" Ross screamed.

" Shut the fuck up. Have some respect," George yelled.

"Let me get my hands on that Nazi bastard," said Ross as he

lunged at Z.

Malone and Jackson blocked Ross from knocking Z senseless as Cummings grabbed him by the lapels and hauled him outside.

"Off you go, sir," he murmured. "You don't want to enrage the men."

On the Mytchett High Street, Captain Cummings ran into Lizzy and her mother shopping. Cummings doffed his hat at the two women.

"Hello, Captain Cummings."

"Hello Lizzy, and this must be your mum."

"Hello, sir. My Lizzy loves looking after Steffi. That's all she talks about," the mother said.

"Well, we love having her, now that Claudia is working full time. I heard you repaired our roof, Lizzy."

Lizzy looked thunderstruck.

"The roof, no, no. Not me, sir."

"We had a major leak in the kitchen and one day it just stopped leaking."

"Oh, that was Claudia, Captain. She's quite the fearless type, I think. Steffi and me, we just helped out with a broom but it was the missus who got up on the roof."

Lizzy noticed the captain's astonished reaction and realized that the cat was out of the bag.

"Sir, I wouldn't know nothin' about stopping a leak in the roof. Your wife's good with a hammer."

"Yes, I imagine she is."

Cummings doffed his hat at the women.

"Good day, Lizzy. Good day, Madam."

Seventeen

Lt Jackson and Lt Malone walked Z around the garden. Near a machine gun pit, Malone waved at the Coldstream Guards who waved back. Z stopped to look at the young men sweating in the June heat and suddenly started off goose-stepping through the garden, giving the men the Nazi salute with the extended arm. Jackson and Malone were dumbstruck. The Coldstream Guards couldn't believe their eyes as they watched the prisoner with growing consternation and hatred.

"Malone, who is that Nazi arsehole?" asked a man.

Jackson and Malone hurried after their prisoner, leaving the soldiers speechless.

"My decision to fly here was influenced by the fact that, among our German leaders, there is the absolute conviction that Britain's position is hopeless," Z said to his visitors.

In the drawing room, Lord Chancellor John Simon smartly dressed in a tailored blue pinstripe suit lit his pipe as he sat near the familiar figure of Ivone Kirkpatrick from the Foreign Office. Z in his Luftwaffe uniform rambled on with talk about German invincibility.

"Our people just keep wondering what on earth can Britain

be hoping for that she keeps on fighting this war," Z said with a cynical air. "All our aircraft plants are still intact and since the war began, many new factories have been completed. Our production has grown so much that we don't know what to do with all the finished airplanes."

"This is all very interesting, Herr Hess, but we need the production figures," Lord Simon said. "Do you know the number of planes being produced by your factories?"

"I know all the factories and Luftwaffe commanders, but I cannot tell you the exact number. I have a good idea of what will happen to Britain sooner or later if we cannot reach a peace settlement."

"Then is your message that in the future there will be a far more violent and terrific attack on Britain?"

"Yes, of course."

Kirkpatrick raised his eyebrows as he glanced at Lord Simon. Obviously, neither man believed a word of this Nazi claptrap.

"Nothing amuses the British people as much as German figures about sinking British tonnage," Lord Simon said. "It makes them laugh."

"Maybe, but I am convinced that the day will come," Z replied, "when English people will no longer laugh about it."

"The day may come, the day may come, Herr Hess," Simon said with a provocative air. "But if your German figures are correct, you know we would all be dead by now."

Lord Simon relit his pipe and formulated a new question.

"*Herr Reichsminister*, might I ask about our bombing of your U-boat yards? We are under the impression that we have bombed your yard at Kiel very successfully."

"You know you can't tell anything from an aerial photograph," Z said. "We have many U-boat yards, sir. Let me assure you, the submarine warfare the Führer is planning hasn't even begun yet."

Kirkpatrick exchanged a look of impatience with Lord Simon.

"*Herr Reichsminister*, I was informed that you had come here with a mission and that you wished to speak of it to someone with government authority. I am the Lord Chancellor and I am ready to discuss with you anything you wish to communicate to our government."

"I am extremely grateful you have come to meet me, Lord Simon. I have come here with a detailed peace plan from the Führer."

Z produced a short one-page handwritten resume of the peace plan and handed it to Kirkpatrick.

"These are the main points."

Kirkpatrick quickly read the plan and looked up.

"There are only 4 points, sir," Kirkpatrick said. "Germany reserves Europe for itself, Germany demands the return of all German colonies, Germany demands full compensation of all German nationals, and Germany will accept the armistice and peace only if it is concluded simultaneously with Italy."

Kirkpatrick looked at Z in disbelief.

"Is that all Herr Hitler wants?" Lord Simon asked.

"It is the Führer's plan, sir. He has mentioned these points to me frequently."

"Well, thank you, Herr Hess," Lord Simon said. "I will communicate your plan to the PM."

Lord Simon and Ivone Kirkpatrick stood up, putting an end to the meeting as Z leaned in close to Lord Simon.

"Can I have a word with you alone, sir?"

Lord Simon nodded to his colleague that he would stay a moment as Kirkpatrick joined Cummings and Dicks in the hallway.

"Lord Simon, I am in danger here," Z whispered after the doors were closed. "I am in fear for my life. I am being poisoned by the guards. They are putting things in my food. Then at night, they are deliberately making noise to prevent me from sleeping."

"Dear man, you must get hold of yourself," Lord Simon said. "You have got this idea that people are interfering with your food. This is fantastic nonsense."

"I always eat from and drink from the common stand but in the morning, I get milk - milk meant only for me - and I get these pains in my stomach."

"You must pull yourself together, old chap, and be brave."

"I got some eggs from Mr Evans down the road," Claudia said. "Now that they are rationed, it will be difficult to find them in the shops.

Cummings watched Claudia spoon food into young Steffi. It was early evening, and they were sitting at the kitchen table having a drink.

"What time do you have to go back?" Claudia asked.

Cummings put down his drink and pulled an ember from the stove, lighting a cigarette.

"In an hour," he said. "I will be working with Martin tonight while Werner is off."

"*Gib Papa einen Kuss.* Give Daddy a kiss. Time for bed, Steffi," Claudia said.

Cummings embraced the child, who followed her mother into the bedroom to get ready for bed. Moments later, Claudia returned to the kitchen and put her arm around Cummings, kissing him on the cheek.

"I met Lizzy and her mum on the High street. She told me Peter Pan repaired our leaky roof," Cumming said.

"Did she now? Peter Pan. What an imagination that girl has!"

"Really, Claudia darling. You could have hurt yourself up there."

Claudia sat in her husband's lap and whispered in his ear.

"*Keine Sorge.* Don't worry, dear. I had my broom with me."

"You are quite the witch, casting spells."

"Watch out, *Liebling.*"

Claudia took a puff from Cummings' cigarette.

"I am going to read a story to Steffi and put her to bed. Before you go, we could..."

Cummings laughed and embraced Claudia.

"Yes, we could darling."

"Don't go away. I will be right back."

Eighteen

It was a particularly noisy night with footsteps on the stairs and a motorcycle courier arriving in the early morning hours. Z paced back and forth as doors banged all over the house and the courier bike roared as it accelerated away.

"*Verdammte Scheiße*," yelled Z angrily, kicking the door and making a terrific racket on the top floor of Mytchett house.

In the basement sound room, Martin wore a headset to monitor the sounds coming from Z's room, and called out to Cummings, who was bunked down for the night in a folded bed.

"Z is up and about, sir. He is yelling and kicking the door."

Cummings woke up slowly, sitting on the edge of the bed and scratching his head.

"Lt Jackson is trying to reason with him, sir."

Cummings looked up at Martin and lit a cigarette.

"He has been going at it most of the night," Martin said. "I can hear him pacing back and forth up there."

Cummings pulled on his shoes.

"I better go up," he said, getting to his feet and leaving the room.

Upstairs in the prisoner's room, Z was sitting on his bed fuming while Jackson tried to reason with him.

"You are waking up the whole bloody house by kicking the door, sir. We can't have that."

"Nobody can sleep in this house, Lieutenant. I must talk to the captain immediately."

"The captain is on duty and cannot leave his post, sir. What do you want? You can tell me."

"I have no trust in you Scots Guards or in the British Secret service. You want to poison me. You want to kill me. I can do nothing to stop you. I must talk to the captain."

Cummings entered the room with a tray holding a cup of tea, a glass of milk, and a piece of *Marmorkuchen*.

"Oh, there you are, Captain. Herr Hess has been asking for you, sir."

"So we are having a little chitchat with the prisoner, Lieutenant?"

"I will leave you to it, sir."

Jackson happily left the captain to deal with the unruly prisoner.

"I've brought you a bit of food and drink, Herr Hess. This should help settle your stomach."

"Thank you for coming, Captain. I have two letters, one addressed to my wife Ilse and the other to the Führer. I want you to have them forwarded through official channels as soon as my death is announced."

Cummings looked stunned by Z's request.

"Your death, sir?"

"Yes, Captain. I don't expect the authorities will allow them to get through, so I have made copies for you."

Cummings put the tray on the table.

"What do you want me to do with the copies?"

"You will wait until the war is over and then you will send them. They will know that I did not take the easy way out. I refused suicide."

Cummings decided it was time to change the subject.

"Why don't you have something to eat?" he asked.

Z nibbled on the *Marmorkuchen*, looking suspiciously at the milk.

"The milk is fine, sir. I poured it myself. Claudia made the *Marmorkuchen*."

"They are trying to kill me, Captain. I cannot take a chance."

Captain Cummings took a sip from the milk.

"Tastes like cow's milk to me, sir. No sweetness or saltiness, nice creamy taste."

Z took the glass from the captain and drank deeply. He then tore into the *Marmorkuchen* with its mottled chocolate and vanilla layers.

"*Sehr gut*, Captain. Tell Claudia the cake is excellent. Will you promise me to send the letters?"

"I will have to talk to my senior officer and Dr Dicks. If they refuse, I will give them back to you. How is that?"

"You are a good friend, Captain. Thank you."

In the morning, Dr Dicks was sitting in the office with a newspaper and a cup of tea when Cummings burst in and threw himself down in a broken chair.

"Doctor, I think we have a problem."

Dicks put down his paper and looked at Cummings.

"I think he may try to kill himself," Cummings said with concern. "He is planning something. He talks about his own death."

"I've heard about the letter to Hitler, Captain. The man is a fool. No one will take him seriously. He's so bloody childish."

"He worries about the food and the sleeping pills. He thinks he's being poisoned."

Dicks looked annoyed but picked up the teapot and poured a cup of tea for Cummings.

"We've heard all this before, Captain. It's a little game he likes to play."

Cummings took the cup and put in milk and sugar. He stirred the tea slowly, trying to collect his thoughts.

"As I understand it, our role is to keep the man happy," Cummings said. "If we can keep him calm, our job will be easier. So, as his physician, I am asking you what we need to do to keep him calm."

"The sleeping pills are sugar pills, placebos, Captain. I have some luminal, a phenobarbitol, which is a sleep inducer, but I haven't given him any yet."

"Why don't you give him the luminal? Maybe that will calm him down. He is going mad up there."

"Let me talk to Colonel Rees. I need to get his permission for the luminal."

Cummings noticed the headline of the newspaper on the desk. It read "PURSUIT OF THE BISMARCK."

"They are still chasing that damn ship."

"You think they will catch the *Bismarck*?" Dicks asked.

"Of course, they will," Cummings said. "After the *Hood* disaster, the PM has put the entire fleet into the chase. He desperately needs a bit of success in the war effort, something to crow about."

Nineteen

"One day Hitler goes to see God. 'I am so happy to see you, Adolf but next time, don't bring that bloke Hermann Göring along with you. Each time he leaves, he takes away a star'," joked Cummings to laughter among the men.

It was a sunny day in the garden, as Malone, Jackson, and Cummings sat with Z at a table overlooking a machine gun pit. On the table was a tea set, a plate of *Rumkugeln* and several newspapers.

"You know, we laugh at Göring in the newsreels with his medals and uniforms," Lt Malone said to Z as he flipped through a copy of Life Magazine.

"So does Göring," Z said. "I know him well. He is a good fellow. The Führer has his own joke about Göring. One day his wife found the *Reichsminister* in the bedroom waving a baton over his underwear on the bed and asked him what he was doing. 'I am promoting my UNDER pants to OVER pants', he replied."

The men broke into a laugh.

"That's a funny story, sir," Cummings said. "Better than mine, I think."

Malone and Jackson looked at a photograph of Hitler and Hess together at the Reichstag and another of Göring, the flamboyant head of the Luftwaffe, addressing a crowd. Dazzled by the Nazi celebrities in the magazine, Jackson asked: "What about Himmler? Did you know him, sir?"

"Himmler is a snake in the grass. I don't know why the Führer puts up with him."

Malone pushed the photograph of Hitler and Hess together at the Reichstag in front of Z.

"Do you remember that day, sir?" Malone asked.

Z looked at the photograph with disdain.

"No, I do not. There are so many pictures of the Führer. I can't remember them all."

Claudia waited in a line of women at the butcher's shop with a canvas bag on her shoulder. A "Share the Meat" poster was taped to the wall showing red meat rations were limited to just 2 ½ lbs per adult per week and 3/4 lb for children under six.

The women presented their ration books to an attractive young Polish butcher with a blond military-style haircut and a pencil mustache. The gregarious young man flirted openly with the elegant young woman just ahead of Claudia.

"That will be four and six pence, miss," he said in heavily accented English.

The woman paid, giving the butcher a come-hither look. She scribbled something on a scrap of paper and handed it to the man. From the smile on his face, it must have been her phone number. The woman picked up her parcel and turned away, avoiding Claudia's glance as she left the shop.

"Next, please."

Claudia stepped forward, and the butcher beamed up the charm.

"I'd like five and three-quarter pounds of minced meat, please."

The butcher reached under the counter and placed a lump of minced meat on the weigh scale. He took his time and gave Claudia a sly, lascivious look before he added to her order of meat. Claudia found the man's attention tiresome.

"There we go, love. That is five and three-quarter pounds. What else can I get you today?"

"That's all, thank you."

The young man wrapped the meat in newsprint and smiled at her.

"I see you are wearing a WAAC uniform, miss. You look very smart in it by the way. Do you work nearby?"

Claudia wanted to laugh at the outrageous flirt but decided to play along.

"Yes, we have only been here a short time."

"You have an accent, I think."

Claudia searched her handbag for the money to pay the man.

"I am Marek, I am Polish from Cracow. You are?"

Claudia smiled as she pocketed her change and started to leave.

"*Ich bin Deutsche aus Köln,*" said Claudia, telling the young man she was from Cologne and challenging him as several local women looked on.

The young Pole froze and looked at her in disbelief.

"You are shocked. You shouldn't be. I work for the British Army and you?"

The young Pole remained speechless. He lifted his hand and touched his chest.

"*Herzgeräusch.* A heart murmur, you know."

His hand shook as he tried to bring it under control.

"*Sie sind ein glücklicher Mann.* You are lucky you are not fighting in North Africa. Good day."

Marek relaxed as Claudia exited the shop. He smiled at the busybodies who considered the foreign talk as tantamount to a crime.

In the mess hall, Captain Cummings, Werner and Z played darts and drank whisky during a quiet afternoon. Claudia appeared from the kitchen and started to wipe down the tables. Several Scots Guards sat in a corner chatting together as the radio played '*There will be Bluebirds over the White Cliffs of Dover*' by Vera Lynn.

"You English think you are so good. We Germans are better at this game."

Z placed his darts neatly in the 20-point section.

"I can see that, sir. You are good and surely improving Werner's game," said Cummings, fawning.

Werner threw his three darts and had trouble hitting the board.

"Werner, you need glasses. Your aim is terrible."

"Maybe I shoot straighter, Captain, if I have another whisky."

The music stopped and the BBC announcer came on.

"The latest news from the British fleet in the North Atlantic. After the retreat of the German battleships *Bismarck* and *Prinz Eugen* to St. Nazaire for repairs, the British fleet took up chase including the aircraft carrier *HMS Ark Royal* and the cruiser *HMS Sheffield*. Some 16 ships participated in the pursuit."

The men listened intently as Cummings prepared to throw a dart.

"As the *Sheffield* engaged the *Bismarck*, Swordfish bombers attacked the German battleship and hit her with two torpedoes, one destroying her port rudder assembly. In the early morning hours, the *HMS King George V* and *HMS Rodney* continued the attack as other ships were obliged to return to port due to fuel shortages. A shell from the *Rodney* blew up the forward bridge and turrets. The *HMS Norfolk* and *HMS Dorsetshire* joined the fray, destroying the *Bismarck*, which burned from stem to stern."

Z looked totally despondent hearing the news, while the others looked quietly jubilant.

"At 10:30 this morning, the *Bismarck* capsized to port and sank. A rescue effort was mounted and then abandoned as U-boats were spotted in the area. British naval sources estimate that the German navy lost some 2,000 men today as the ship sank. The sinking of the *Bismarck* is a major victory for the British Navy after the recent losses in the Eastern Mediterranean. Now back to our programme."

The Scots Guards suddenly jumped up and down with loud hurrahs and did a jig around the tables. After so many military disasters, there was a feeling of euphoria and deep relief among the Englishmen in the room. The voices got louder and louder and broke out spontaneously across Camp Z from machine gun pit to machine gun pit.

"WE SANK THE BISMARCK, WE SANK THE BISMARCK..."

Werner emerged from the kitchen with a bottle of brandy and a dozen small glasses. He filled the glasses to the brim as the men were swept up in the celebration. Looking glum, Z retreated to his room, reluctantly followed by Malone.

Off-duty Scots Guards started to fill the mess hall, drinking from flasks and purloined bottles of whisky amid cries of "WE SANK THE BISMARCK" and "VICTORY OVER GERMANY."

Twenty

In the prisoner's room, Werner put the shortwave radio on the table next to Z's books. He plugged it in and played with the antenna as Z watched him from the chair near the window.

Captain Cummings had consented to Z's request for a radio in the hope that the radio would help the prisoner pass the time and perhaps keep his mind off any plans of suicide.

"*Claudia und ich kommen aus Trent Park, Herr Hess.* We come from Trent Park. There are a lot of German officers to feed over there."

Z watched Werner silently.

"They like Claudia's cakes and our German food."

"What is this Trent Park?"

"It is a camp for German officers, sir. It's very select."

Werner tuned the radio, looking for German radio broadcasts, stopping on a weak signal from *Soldatensender Belgrad*, which was playing *Lili Marlene* by Lale Andersen.

> "*Vor der Kaserne, vor dem großen Tor*
> *stand eine Laterne*
> *und steht sie noch davor,*
> *so woll'n wir da uns wiedersehn,*
> *bei der Laterne woll'n wir stehn*

wie einst Lili Marleen,
wie einst Lili Marleen."

"This is *Soldatensender Belgrad*, sir. German forces radio in Yugoslavia. You like?"

Z said nothing as he listened to the song. Werner left the room to go downstairs just as Claudia climbed the stairs with a plate of *Windbeutel,* similar to cream puffs, on a tray. She stopped in the doorway, captivated by the German song on the radio. After a moment, she entered the room.

"I have brought you a *windbeutel,* Herr Hess."

Z looked at Claudia with tears in his eyes.

"*Moin, moin, Claudia. Vielen Dank.* Thank you, Claudia."

"*Bitte schön.* It's a pleasure, sir. The song brings back memories."

"Yes, it does. Where are you from, Claudia?"

"I am from Cologne."

Claudia handed the plate to Z.

"*Köln* is a wonderful city," Z said as he bit into the cream puff. "Do you still love your homeland, Claudia?"

"I love the Germany of my youth, sir. I love the songs and the music."

"*Ja, in der Tat, Claudia.* Yes, indeed."

Claudia wiped a tear from her eye and left silently as *Lili Marlene* continued to play on the radio.

In the basement sound room, Cummings, Claudia and Werner drank their ersatz coffee around the table during the afternoon debriefing.

"'*Moin, moin*' is a Hamburgisch expression for 'Good Morning', Paul," Claudia explained. "Maybe Bremen, Kiel, a

Plattdeutsch dialect from Northern Germany."

Cummings was skeptical, not having Claudia's ear for German accents.

"Are you sure he said that?" Cummings asked.

"I heard it, but it was very faint. I could be mistaken," added Werner.

"I am sure he said it. I was in the room. It startled me. What else could it be?" Claudia insisted.

"No one from Bavaria would ever say that, Captain. Hess wouldn't be familiar with it," Werner said.

"Good, we are making progress. Anything else, Werner?"

"He enjoys the radio, sir."

"Excellent. The radio will be useful. I am happy the Foreign Office is allowing it."

"He is a romantic, Paul, an easy mark for us," Claudia said.

"He was very curious about Trent Park," Werner said. "He can't fathom why we are baking cakes for German officers. He must think we are quite mad."

Claudia smiled at Werner.

"It's amazing," Claudia added. "None of the German officers over there seems to suspect we might be listening in to their conversations. They enjoy their drinks in the garden and the club atmosphere, as if there were no longer a war going on."

Cummings looked preoccupied by the mission.

"You must be very careful, Werner. Don't lead the conversation. Let Z ask the questions. Keep your distance. Show a lack of interest. If he gets suspicious, we will have lost him."

"Of course, Captain."

"Paul, don't worry. He is an easy mark, totally unsophisticated. We are making real progress." Claudia said with assurance.

After lunch Claudia knocked on Z's door to collect the tray. Z was at his desk ostensibly reading a book in German as he slipped several pills into an envelope for future analysis. He hid the envelope behind the book.

"*Guten Tag,*" said Z as Claudia took away the tray.

"It's a lovely day for a walk, sir."

"You see these pills, Claudia? These are the sleeping pills Dr Dicks gave me. They don't make me sleep, they have the opposite effect. They keep me awake all night long."

"I am sorry, sir. Have you talked to Dr Dicks?"

"Many times. He ignores my complaints."

"Well, I think you should stop taking them, sir. Maybe you will sleep better."

"*Ja, gut.* I will do that."

Z returned to his reading as Claudia left with the tray.

"I love a martini, darling. Where did you get the gin?" Cummings asked.

"Black market," Claudia grinned, playing with the olive in her drink. "I can't reveal the source."

They were sitting outside in the yard on a warm summer evening, watching Steffi as she played in the sandpit with a tin bucket. A glass cocktail shaker sat incongruously on a wooden milk crate.

"It is very good for a homemade brew," Cummings said. "What about the vermouth?"

"Fortified wine, my dear. Just a whiff of it and, of course, crushed ice. Mr Evans is such a darling, he brought me the wine and the ice."

"Evans is quite amazing."

"I was at the butcher's the other day when this Polish chap from Cracow asked me about my accent," Claudia sipped from her martini. "The man is a terrible flirt. He is very handsome and must be running a harem by now with all the men off to war. Some of the women were passing him slips of paper with their telephone numbers. It was disgraceful."

"Why is a Pole working in a butcher's shop?"

"He says he's got a *herzgeräusch*."

"A heart murmur. So I reckon he doesn't qualify to serve in the Polish Army," Cummings said.

"Anyway, he asked me about my accent. I almost replied what accent. I felt so alone with all those proper English ladies watching us and me, a foreigner in an English butcher's shop with a war going on. I couldn't reply in English, not with all those women listening in, so I spoke to him in German and he froze. It was almost comical."

"You could always have ignored him, said nothing."

"Yes, I could have ignored him, but he was so bloody irritating, coming on to me like that."

Cummings smiled and reached over to top up her glass.

"I think you want to get me drunk."

"Of course, I do. What else did the man say?"

"Not much. I told him I worked for the British Army. Then he mentioned he had a *herzgeräusch*."

"He used that term, or did he say heart murmur?"

"He spoke in German."

Cummings' suspicions were aroused and his face took on a concerned look.

"What?" Claudia asked.

"Oh, I don't know. You are very attractive in that WAAC

uniform. Maybe it was just a flirtation? Did he strike up a conversation with anyone else?"

"He was talking to all the women."

"A German-speaking Pole in a butcher's shop might raise a flag or two. I will have a talk with the senior officer at Mytchett and see what he says."

"It was probably nothing," Claudia said, raising her glass to her husband.

"Cheers, *Liebling*."

Twenty-one

Dr Dicks entered the room and found Z drinking whisky at the table in front of a mess of books and papers.

"I can't sleep, Doctor."

Dicks pulled a small bottle of pills from his suit pocket.

"I am going to give you something different tonight. Some luminal will put you to sleep, but you shouldn't be drinking whisky with this pill. Who gave you the whisky?"

"The captain gave me the bottle."

Dicks took several capsules of luminal from the bottle and gave one to Z.

"*Bitte, geben sie Sie mir, Herr Doktor.* Give them to me, Doctor. I am being undone and you know it."

Dicks looked curiously at Z as he put the pill bottle away.

"What do you mean undone, Herr Hess? You look all right to me. All you need is a good night's sleep."

"You know what I mean, Doctor."

"Try to get some sleep. It is very late, tomorrow you'll feel better. We'll talk again."

Z watched Dicks leave and slipped the luminal pill into his mouth.

An hour before dawn, Z lay wide-awake on his bed with a crazed look on his face. He tried to get up, but soon fell to the floor as the room started to swing left and right. The hallucinations were so real that he sensed the wall moving towards him and crushing him against the bed frame. He scrambled to protect his legs and lost consciousness, lying naked on the floor.

Germany, February 1941

In a ruined village near the Oder River, an unshaven Z in scruffy clothing and a forage cap wandered aimlessly through his family home. The front door had been ripped off, and a goat bolted through the open door almost running into Z as he stepped inside.

He looked around the kitchen and dining area with its smashed chairs and broken china. He walked through the house to the back and looked out at an overgrown garden through a cracked window. He stepped outside.

In the distance, Z saw the smoking ruins of a neighbour's house. He walked along a row of turnips and pulled one out of the hard ground. He stood up and nibbled on the turnip. The tangy taste brought back memories of long, happy summers.

Mytchett 1941

Lt Malone entered the prisoner's room with the breakfast tray and found Z slumped in the corner, naked. He couldn't tell if he was unconscious or not. He pulled the drapes aside to admit some light and leaned over Z for a closer look.

"Sir, are you all right?"

Z groaned but wouldn't get up.

"Let me help you," Malone said, reaching for Z's arm.

Z screamed something incomprehensible in German and shoved the lieutenant away. Malone stared angrily at Z for a moment, then turned on his heel and left the room. He hurried downstairs and knocked on Dr Dick's office door. He entered to find Dicks working on a report at his desk.

"He has gone crazy, sir. He is lying naked on the floor. Can you come up, please?"

"Yes, of course."

Together, Dicks and Malone went upstairs. In the prisoner's room, they found Z holding his head after having vomited on the floor.

"He may simply be feeling under the weather due to the sleeping pill," said Dicks, looking down at the prisoner groaning on the floor.

"Let's get him back to bed. Give me a hand, Lieutenant."

They grabbed his arms and dragged him back to bed.

"You think he is sick because he caught something, Doctor?" Captain Cummings asked.

Cummings and Malone were in the mess hall having lunch with Dicks.

"I don't see what he could have caught. He has had nothing special to eat," Dicks said.

"You started him on the luminal. Maybe it's a reaction to the luminal?"

"Impossible. I gave him just the one pill on Colonel Rees' orders. It can't be the luminal. It's a sleep inducer, it won't harm him."

"He won't eat anything, sir. He sits on the floor and won't talk." Malone added.

Cummings looked at Dicks and hated the arrogant prick with his pompous manners and old school vanity.

"Well, Doctor. You are the medical man, so what's the fucking prognosis?"

Irritated by Cummings' vulgarity, Dicks replied in his usual clipped monotone.

"We need to keep a close watch on him. If it is a psychosis, he may very well attempt to cut himself, to self-mutilate, he may become aggressive or even try to kill himself."

"Jesus Christ, I think we should bring in Major Foley for a consultation. He isn't sick, but you think he might top himself."

Dicks put down his spoon, crossed his arms and looked at Cummings with a serious air.

"Captain, do you want my opinion on the matter? I am the physician in charge here. It is my responsibility. I have had dozens of patients in a similar state and they all emerged unscathed."

"Unscathed? Do you mean they were all catatonic? Is that what you mean, Doctor?" Cummings asked with a cynical air.

"By unscathed, I mean they all got over it."

"I am worried about your patient, Doctor. We have a vested interest in the health of this man. If he were to self-mutilate or try to kill himself, the consequences would be too bloody awful to contemplate."

"Of course, I am concerned, but I think the best thing to do is to let him rest for the moment. He may come out of it all by himself in the next day or two. I will go up this evening and try to calm him."

Cummings shook his head in frustration. He thought about

how easily his mission would be compromised if Z continued down this slippery slope.

Twenty-two

Marek stood in the lane leading to the stable house. He wore his Polish military uniform and looked around briefly before walking brazenly into the yard. He knocked out a pane of glass in the back door and reached inside for the door handle. He slipped inside the house.

Marek entered the living room and glanced briefly at a few papers on the coffee table. He went into the master bedroom and opened the chest of drawers. He ran his hand under Claudia's underwear and rifled through the other drawers quickly, moving on to the bedside table.

He rummaged through the papers in the dustbin just as a knock came at the front door. He jumped up and ran back through the hall, observing a man in overalls and a beret peering through the window. He hesitated a moment and then went to the door, opening it.

"Is the missus in?" the man asked.

"No, sir. She is out. Can I help you?"

"You are?" the man looked at him suspiciously.

"I am a friend of the family," Marek said confidently, with a smirk.

"My name is Evans. Tell her I will have the eggs and meat next Monday."

"Of course, sir."

"The captain has a lovely family. Claudia and young Steffi, they need quality victuals. I'll be on my way, young man. You are with the Polish Army?"

"You are quite right, sir."

"Good luck to you. You Poles are helping us win this bloody war."

Evans turned quickly and climbed on his three-wheel bike, loaded with orders to deliver up and down the lane.

In the prisoner's room, Z was still on the floor, slipping in and out of consciousness.

"How are you feeling, Herr Hess?" Dr Dicks asked, squatting near the prisoner.

Z groaned briefly and drifted away.

"I can't help you if you won't help yourself. Would you like some food?" Dicks said.

There was no reply as Lt Jackson entered the room.

"This place stinks. I think he peed on the floor, sir."

"We'll have it cleaned up, Lieutenant. He will come around soon. Let's get him back to bed."

"I'll get a mop in here right after lunch."

"Good man."

Dicks and Jackson picked up the unconscious prisoner and hauled him back to bed, covering him with blankets. Hess groaned briefly as his tormented mind worked overtime.

Germany, February 1941

In the ruined village, Z stepped around a broken bicycle in

the yard and imagined his mother hanging laundry on the washing line. Frau Hörner was a large woman in an apron and scarf, and with pockets full of clothespins.

"*Sei vorsichtig mit dem Fahrrad, Max,*" Frau Hörner warned the child who approached along the path, wobbling dangerously from side to side on his bike, as he passed Z and disappeared under the washing line.

A gunshot was heard, and the illusion was broken. Z returned to the present and saw *Obersturmbannführer* Richter in his black SS uniform, step out into the garden from the back door and order him to come back.

"*Kommen Sie zurück.*"

Z looked at the empty wasteland of ruined houses and suddenly felt short of breath and dizzy. His heartbeat accelerated, and he had trouble breathing. He started back towards the house but slumped down into the long grass. Richter approached as Z writhed on the ground, curled up in the fetal position with his eyes closed.

"*Sind Sie krank?*" asked Richter, thinking Z was sick.

"*Ich fühle mich schlecht. Mir geht es nicht gut,*" murmured Z, having a panic attack.

Richter looked down angrily at Z and kicked him hard in the ribs, ordering him to stand up.

"*Aufstehen Faulpelz. Aufstehen.*"

Cummings peeked through the spyhole. Z looked quite mad lying on the bed and making faces at something in the corner of the room. He had not touched the food on the table. He yelled an order to the imaginary character in the room: "*Mach schnell.*"

In the adjoining room , Cummings allowed Jackson to take

a peek at the prisoner through the spyhole.

"What do you think, Captain?"

"I think he's sodding mad. He's gone psycho on us. I only hope Dicks knows what he's doing."

After a long silence, Jackson observed Z glaring at someone with a crazed look and yelling: "*Raus hier!*"

"What time do you start the oven, Werner?" Lt Malone asked.

It was well after midnight as the two men sat outside on the front porch having a smoke.

"Around seven," Werner replied. "We let the dough rise before it goes in the oven."

"Do you like making bread?"

Werner turned to Malone and smiled.

"You know, Lieutenant. It is my greatest pleasure, my hands working the dough and then watching the bread rise. I think of my mother. She was like me with bread, making challah for the Shabbat meal."

Malone smiled at Werner as a motorcycle courier arrived at the guardhouse, handed an envelope to a soldier, and then headed back out, gunning the engine.

"Never underestimate the importance of small tasks, Lieutenant," Werner said. "They can bring the greatest joy."

"My mum used to say that a lot, out on the Canadian prairies. Milking cows, shovelling shit, putting up fences, you name it. Small jobs bring the greatest of joy!"

"You sound a bit cynical, I would say, Lieutenant."

Werner took a silver flask from his inside pocket and offered it to Malone.

"Want a nip of French brandy, Lieutenant, to keep out the

chill?"

"Thanks, Werner. I hope you don't mind me asking, but I think you are working on the Q. T. with the captain?"

"I go where the captain sends me, Lieutenant. That's all I can tell you."

Z was lying in bed naked when he heard the sound of the motorcycle in the courtyard. He stumbled over to the door and started banging on it with his fists.

Lt Jackson rushed into the room.

"It's late, sir. Everyone is trying to sleep."

'Die Kameraden kommen',' Z yelled and started to bang on the wall. Jackson swore at the man, grabbing his arm to prevent him from making further noise.

"Do you want to talk to Dicks, Mr Hess? I will go get him, but please stop making noise."

Jackson sat Z down on the bed and left the room, leaving the door open. Z looked briefly into the corner of the room, his face frozen in a rictus of repulsion. The gruff voice of Herr Oberst sounded in his head.

"Nutzen Sie die Gelegenheit, Soldat. Seize the occasion and escape from this prison."

Z started to pull on his pants and flying boots, and slipped into his Luftwaffe uniform.

"Dress smartly, soldier."

Z turned towards the door.

"Nutzen Sie die Gelegenheit!"

As the voice of Herr Oberst faded away, Z stood up and went to the door to listen to the sound of footsteps on the stairs.

In his dressing gown, Dicks climbed the stairs followed by

Jackson. As they arrived on the landing after clearing the gate, Z burst out of his room running for the stairs. He leapt into the air, clearing the stairwell balustrade and dropped out of sight to the floor below.

All at once, pandemonium broke loose as Dicks, followed by Jackson, opened the gate again with a key and ran down the stairs yelling at the night staff coming up from the kitchen. "Don't shoot him. Please don't shoot him."

Twenty-three

Berlin 1973

"I thought that was the end of it," Cummings said. "We had accomplished nothing. Z had a fractured leg. MI6 was up in arms."

At the *biergarten*, Cummings was working on his second stein and had ordered another for Terry.

"Major Foley called 'C' in London, requesting a surgeon specialist. They sent Major Murray from the Royal College of Surgeons, who splinted the leg and gave him an injection. 'Mum's the word' was the message from Major Foley. We went back to work the next day as if nothing had happened."

"Why didn't they move him out of there?" Terry asked.

Lost in his memories, Cummings suddenly turned to Terry and raised his glass, toasting the good doctor.

"Cheers, Dr Terry. What a lovely afternoon!"

"Cheers," Terry replied, lifting his stein.

"Well, you know how things were during the war. We were told to make do and manage the situation. The PM's office simply decided to keep it under wraps. I don't really blame them. We were at war and the well-being of Z was not a priority."

Mytchett 1941

Bedridden with his leg in a plaster cast, Z was busy sketching some flowers in a vase with a pencil when Claudia entered the room to pick up the tray.

"*Guten Tag*. How are you today?"

Z said nothing, continuing his sketch.

"There is another letter from Frau Hess, sir. I will put it on the table."

Claudia put the letter bearing numerous war department stamps on the table and suddenly noticed the profusion of maybugs congregating on the drapes and the books. It reminded her of her childhood.

"*Woher kommen all diese Maikäfer?* The maybugs? Where do they come from?"

"*Ich weiß nicht,*" Z replied. "Maybe the garden."

Claudia picked up a maybug in the palm of her hand and recited a nursery rhyme as she examined the insect.

"*Maikäfer, flieg.*
Der Vater ist im Krieg.
Die Mutter ist in Pommerland.
Und Pommerland ist abgebrannt.
Maikäfer, flieg!"

(Maybug, fly away.
Father's in the war.
Mother's in Pomerania.
Pomerania's all burnt down.
Maybug, fly away.)

Claudia blew the maybug off her hand through the open window and picked up the tray.

"*Das ist ein wunderbares Wiegenlied,* Claudia. That's a wonderful nursery rhyme. Please say the words again."

"If you like, sir."

Claudia repeated the words.

"*Maikäfer, flieg.*

Der Vater ist im Krieg..."

Z listened intently, captivated by the words. There was a long silence before he spoke again.

"*Meine Mutter hat es mir vorgesungen* .My mother would sing it. She came from Rostock."

"*Ihre Mutter?* What is her name?"

"Frieda."

"You know the English have their own version:
'Ladybug, ladybug, fly away home,
Your house is on fire and your children are gone.'"

Z laughed and clapped his hands.

"You know, Claudia, this is the first time I hear about this English 'Ladybug'."

"*Möchten sie eine Rumkugeln, Herr Hess.* Would you like a chocolate rum ball?"

"*Ja, bitte.*"

Claudia left with the tray to fetch the *Rumkugeln.*

Cummings and Claudia congregated around Martin in the sound room while they listened to the playback of Z's voice recording. Through a load of static, they heard Claudia's reciting of the *Maikäfer* nursery rhyme.

"You are incredible, Claudia. You have charmed the man," Martin said, laughing.

"He is not alone, young fellow," Cummings said with a smile.

Claudia laughed as Martin turned off the recording.

"Rudolf's mother, Klara Münch, came from Hof in Bavaria, not Rostock," Claudia said.

"It gives us a locus," Cummings added. "We should be able to work out the rest of his story."

"Have you seen him at the dinner table, Paul?" Claudia asked. "With his table manners, I don't think Z comes from a rich family. Perhaps he was a factory worker or a farm labourer."

"Suppose for a moment that the SS recruited him," Cummings proposed. "They picked him up off the street because he looked like Hess and thought he might be useful."

"Yes, I would think that is how it happened," Claudia replied.

Cummings continued thinking out loud.

"Anyone travelling with a face like that would attract immediate attention. They had to keep him under wraps, isolated, in a secret location. No one can know they have the perfect double for the *Reichsminister*. Bearing that in mind, how would they handle his training, do you think?"

"They would bring in a team of people from Berlin, Paul," Claudia said. "All of them sworn to secrecy."

"Yes, I agree and they would keep him locked up where they found him," Cummings replied. "The local unit would be in charge. The fewer people in the know, the better."

"His English is very good. He knows the idiom better than I do," Claudia said. "So they would have to bring in an English teacher from Berlin or Hamburg, and it would take a good deal of time to train him."

"He would also have to learn everything there is to know

about Hess," Martin said. "That would mean a team of teachers, not just a language coach."

"Yes, you are right," Cummings said. "Clearly a team of professionals."

Cummings was silent for a moment.

"You know this kind of thing takes serious planning and money - training a decoy and sending him into enemy territory. I am thinking of the time it would take."

"It would take months, perhaps a full year, Paul," Claudia added.

Cummings pulled a file from his briefcase.

"Major Foley estimates he had less than 50 hours of flight training. So his departure for Scotland may have been precipitated. Let's check the flying schools in the area. Neukuhren in East Prussia, the Luftkriegschule2 at Gatow, the Schleswig Jagel airbase where they fly the Me110s."

"If you were training a man like Z to fly, would you want him at a flight school with large numbers of young men who might notice him, Paul? I don't think so," Claudia added.

"Maybe he was trained at a factory," Martin said. "A Messerschmitt factory. Remember, the guns were still packed in grease."

"Right, very good point, Martin. I think I have a list of factories building the Messerschmitt planes. Let's take a look."

"At 4 o'clock this morning, Hitler attacked and invaded Russia," said Churchill over the radio in the mess hall. "This was no surprise to me. In fact, I gave clear and precise warnings to Stalin of what was coming."

Captain Cummings was having lunch with Lt Malone and Lt Jackson next to a group of Scots Guards. The men were silent as they listened to the news.

"Hitler is a monster of wickedness, insatiable in his lust for blood and plunder," continued Churchill in a sombre tone. "Not content with having all Europe under his heel, or else terrorized into various forms of abject submission, he must now carry his work of butchery and desolation among the vast multitudes of Russia and of Asia."

"What does this mean, Captain?" Malone asked.

"This is the very best news we have heard in over a year, Lieutenant," Cummings replied.

Claudia and Werner drifted in from the kitchen as the BBC news report continued. A moment later, Dr Dicks joined them.

"The German Wehrmacht supported by Finnish, Slovak, Hungarian, Romanian and Italian units swept into the Russian heartland today on a front extending from the Arctic circle to the Crimea."

Dicks looked stunned and said: "If German forces are attacking the Red Army. It means they won't be invading Britain anytime soon."

"This is incredible news, Malone!" Cummings said. "We were expecting an invasion across the English channel. Now, Hitler has clearly abandoned his plans and is going after Stalin. He will try to succeed where Napoleon failed!"

Twenty-four

"The door was wide open when I arrived. I locked it before I left," Claudia said.

Cummings was on his knees, examining the broken window pane near the back door of the stable house. Claudia sat with Steffi, who was eating her supper at the kitchen table.

"Are you sure they didn't take anything, darling?" Cummings asked.

"Everything seems to be here. If they were after jewellery, they didn't take any of my things. I have my grandmother's ring, which is quite valuable, but it wasn't touched."

"Maybe they didn't have time to steal anything. I will drop by the police station and report the incident in the morning."

"I mentioned the break-in to Lizzy and she couldn't believe it. People don't lock their doors in Mytchett."

"I find it rather surprising, but perhaps someone saw us leave the house and wondered whether they might find something to nick," Cummings said.

At the entrance to Mytchett House, Cummings met a young man in a military uniform carrying a briefcase.

"You must be Lieutenant Morley. I have been expecting

you."

"Yes, sir. Are you Captain Cummings?"

"Yes, Lieutenant. Let's go up."

As they climbed the stairs to the prisoner's room, they heard German military marches blaring from the radio. They entered the prisoner's room and found Z sitting on the bed with his leg in a plaster cast, looking at a book with pictures of English country houses. Cummings crossed to the radio and turned it down before presenting Morley to Z.

"This is Lt Morley, sir. He is here to check your vision for the new spectacles."

"*Sehr gut.* I can't see much with the old ones."

"Can I see them, sir?"

Z removed his old glasses and handed them to Morley.

"Thank you. I will set up over here if you don't mind, sir."

Z nodded his agreement as Cummings took a seat at the table. Morley pulled out a Snellen chart from his briefcase and fixed it to the wall near the door.

"Have you heard the news, Captain?"

Z pointed to the headlines of *The Times* on the table.

"The invasion of Russia. Yes, I have," Cummings said.

"This is the largest invasion in the history of mankind. Only the Führer could have done this. The newspaper said that three million German soldiers had attacked the Soviet devil. They will be invincible. They will take Moscow within a month, then they will turn their attention on Britain."

Cummings frowned at this pro-German interpretation of the news, but decided to sound encouraging.

"I am sure you are right. We will not be spared by the invincible Nazi war machine. How is your leg today?"

"It gets better every day, Captain. They are taking off the plaster cast tomorrow."

Morley stood by the eye chart with a large 'E' at the top and called to Z.

"Now, sir. I would like you to stand near the bed."

Z stood up on his good leg near the bed, happy to accommodate the captain and Morley.

"Yes, that is good. Step back a foot or two, please. That's about 20 feet. Now, cover your left eye and read the third line with your right."

"T-O-Z," the prisoner read.

"Very good," Morley said. "Now the fifth line."

"E-F-B-P."

Z made several errors and obviously needed glasses to read the line correctly.

"Thank you, sir. Now, cover your right eye and read the third line with your left."

"These men are communists and criminals," Z declared. "We must lock them up. We cannot let them plot against the state."

Z was looking at a book about a German concentration camp in Austria that Dr Dicks had provided. The documentation came from Wilton Park and was used to re-educate POWs.

Dicks, Jackson and Z were having *Kaffee und Kuchen* (coffee and cake) in the garden near a machine gun pit. Z reclined in a lounge chair without his plaster cast.

"What do you think is the purpose of these camps?" Dicks asked.

"You should know, you British invented them during the Boer War. We Germans are simply following your example."

Dicks popped a *Rumkugeln* into his mouth as Z continued

his tirade on concentration camps.

"With your record in Ireland, India and Palestine, you have not earned the right to accuse anyone," Z said. "We would never send women and children to our concentration camps. That is something we would never do. When I get back to Germany, I will try to find out whether our people have done this against the will of the leadership."

Dicks handed Z the plate of *Rumkugeln*.

"Please have one, Herr Hess."

"*Vielen Dank, Herr Doktor.*"

He slipped a *Rumkugeln* into his mouth.

"I have heard that your colleague Joseph Goebbels has had your picture removed from the walls of office buildings and schools in Germany," Dicks said. "Streets named after you have been renamed. I don't think you would be well advised to return to Germany any time soon, sir."

Z looked flabbergasted.

"The Führer would not permit it. No, that is impossible."

Dicks smiled, having put a hole in Z's hot air balloon of lies and misplaced pride.

"It is time you accept the reality of your situation, Herr Hess. In Germany, you are a non-person, a traitor to the fatherland. Only yesterday a hospital named after you was re-christened."

"That is not possible. I am the Führer's closest friend. They would never dare."

Captain Cummings arrived and signalled to Dicks to come with him. Dicks stood up to leave.

"Captain, do you agree I am the Führer's best friend?" Z asked.

"I am sure the Führer misses you, sir. But I read in the papers that Martin Bormann has taken over your old job and has been nominated as head of the *Parteikanzlei* (Party Chancellery)."

Z was enraged at the thought of an underling usurping his power back home.

"Before I forget, I have your new spectacles with me."

Cummings removed a small case from his pocket and handed it to Z who admired his new pair of spectacles. He slipped the round eyeglasses over his nose and looked at the captain.

"How is your sight now, Herr Hess?" Dicks asked.

"It is a big improvement. Amazing. Thank you, Captain."

Dicks and Cummings left Jackson in charge of Z and returned to the house, where they joined Claudia and Werner around the coffee table in the drawing room.

"Sorry to drag you away from a pleasant afternoon in the garden," Cummings said to Dicks.

"What is it, Captain?" Dicks asked with concern.

"I was over at the police station earlier and they are looking for a Polish man who killed a butcher on the High Street in Mytchett. This is the same man who Claudia talked to last week at the shop. He goes by the name of Marek. He speaks German. He has been seen wearing a Polish uniform. We think he may be a German agent."

"So what are the military police doing to catch this man?" Dicks asked.

"I have no idea. Yesterday we had a break-in at our house, but nothing was stolen."

"Have you talked to Major Foley?"

"Yes, I was on the phone with him this morning. The major thinks this man may have been working with the three German parachutists who were arrested near Luton Hoo and planned to attack the interrogation centre at Cockfosters. He thinks this man may be sniffing around Camp Z looking for information about Hess. We are all potential targets, so I want you to watch your backs. The man is obviously very dangerous."

"How do you know he is Polish?" Werner asked.

"We don't. All we know is that he spoke briefly in German to Claudia in the shop. He said he had a *herzgeräusch* to explain why he wasn't eligible to serve."

"A *herzgeräusch*. Not many Poles would know that word, Captain," Dicks said.

"Few, if any, I would think."

"I don't think he is Polish, Paul. He may be German or even Russian." Claudia said.

"We need to keep an eye out for him. He may still be in the vicinity wearing a Polish uniform."

Twenty-five

Claudia was alone in the kitchen, feeding young Steffi. She got up to pour a glass of milk for the child and looked out the window at the young policeman standing guard in the front lane. She went to the back door and checked that it was locked before returning with the milk.

A knock came at the front door as Claudia put a glass of milk in front of Steffi. She went to open the door.

"Mr Evans, come in. How are you?"

Evans, in dirty overalls and sporting a beret, stepped over the threshold and thrust a package into Claudia's hands.

"Good day, ma'am. Here are your eggs and meat."

"I wasn't expecting you today."

"That's all right, love."

Claudia took the package and removed several coins from her purse. She handed them to Evans.

"I did tell the young man Monday, ma'am."

"Young man?"

"Yes, the bloke who was here. The Polish chap in uniform."

Claudia suddenly looked terrified.

"Are you all right, ma'am? Did I say something?"

"You saw a man in the house. When was this, Mr Evans, please?"

"Well, last week. I popped by and rang the bell. The young man came to the door. A nice bloke, as I said."

"The Polish butcher. He killed a man last week in Mytchett, Mr Evans."

"No, no. This was a young man, a nice lad. You must be mistaken."

"The police are looking for this man. They think he is a German agent."

Evans' arms dropped to his sides, and he looked stunned.

"Please, come in Mr Evans. Let me make you a cup of tea. I am just now feeding Steffi. She will enjoy seeing you."

In his room, Z was busy writing a letter to his wife Ilse, carefully forming the letters in longhand. The table in front of him was littered with his notes and some of Ilse's earlier letters.

"Meine liebe Ilse,
I am sorry to hear about your difficulties of the past months. I have been ill now for quite some time after receiving drugs and various poisons in my food, and I could not write. I am happy to hear about the boy. You must learn to control your desire to keep him safe because school is so very important in the lives of boys."

Z listened to footsteps in the hall and then continued writing as he consulted his notes.

"Those who cram their way to the top of their class get there by swotting and not through any intellectual gift, and they are usually the ones who disappoint most in later life. I wish my son only one thing in life: that some idea shall 'fire' him - an engineering design, or a new concept in medicine, or a drama - even if nobody is willing to build his engine or to stage or even read his drama and the doctors of every faculty come down on him in rare unanimity to tear his ideas to shreds."

A knock came at the door, and Werner stepped into the room.

"*Guten Morgen, Herr Hess*. Lt Malone said your radio wasn't working properly. Do you want me to take a look?"

Annoyed by the interruption, Z stopped writing and put his letter away.

"I think there is something wrong with the tuning."

"I will take it with me if you don't mind, sir."

Werner unplugged the radio and removed it.

"So, Werner, who do the British have locked up at Trent Park?" Z asked.

"I wouldn't know, sir. They are officers, all of them. They've even got a few important generals, I heard."

"So they eat well, do they?"

"The very best food and drink. It is part of the British welcome for Luftwaffe and U-boat officers."

"Luftwaffe officers? I don't understand why they do this?"

"Well, sir. I think they hope to turn the officers, you know. Make friends with them and perhaps recruit them for the RAF in the far East."

"How do you know that?"

"I talked to a pilot from the 10th Airborne regiment from Neukuhren. He said that the Luftwaffe has the best pilots in the world and the British want them."

Z was stunned to hear of such treason.

"He told you the name of his regiment and his base in Neukuhren?"

"Of course, sir."

"It is against the rules for any flier to give the name of his regiment. I will have a word with Herr Göring when I return."

Werner headed for the door with the radio and stopped momentarily to say a final word.

"*Sie haben viel Spaß*. They are having great fun. The war is over for those poor blokes. They are safe here. They prefer to serve in the RAF than go to an internment camp. But I hear you are a pilot, too."

"Yes, I am a pilot."

"Maybe the RAF will hire you, too. Would you like a drink before lunch, sir?"

At the stable house, Cummings showed a police inspector the broken window. The inspector was a short man with a narrow foxy face who talked out of the side of his mouth.

"Captain, why would our man be coming around here?"

"I have no idea, sir."

Cummings and the inspector entered the kitchen, where Claudia was clearing away the dirty dishes as Steffi played in a corner.

"I don't see why he broke into your house," the inspector said. "There are many more attractive houses in the lane for a crook if you are looking for things to nick."

Claudia appeared annoyed by the questions.

"We think he may be a German agent, Inspector," Claudia said. "That's what German agents do. They sneak around."

The inspector lit his pipe, taking his time.

"Evans saw the man, ma'am. He described him to a T. You

think he is a German agent?"

Claudia and Paul exchanged a look.

"We can't be sure about anything, inspector," Cummings said. "He may be a German agent or just Polish riffraff who noticed Claudia in the butcher's shop and came after her."

"I have my doubts, Captain. The man we are looking for is a professional assassin. The way he killed the butcher was particularly sadistic, making his victim suffer the way he did."

Claudia looked frightened and quickly left the room with Steffi.

Twenty-six

"*Sie haben viel Spaß.* Werner, really. He must think Trent House is an asylum for the mentally deranged," Claudia said as Werner entered the basement sound room wearing a kitchen apron.

"Ha, ha. You are right, Claudia."

Claudia held up the letter she'd been reading.

"I need you to take a look at his letter to Ilse, Werner. Perhaps you will see something."

Werner took the letter and sat down to read. Nearby, Martin was monitoring the sound from microphones placed throughout the house.

"He is quite clever," Werner said. "He gets by the censors by sending out a copy of his last letter with each new letter."

"The censors never remember from one day to the next what was blue-pencilled," Claudia said.

"I have been thinking, Claudia. You know, a man with a face like his."

"Yes."

"If Z was my baby, I would want to test him to see whether he could pass for Rudolf Hess in a public forum. Put him next to Herman Göring or Robert Ley on a podium."

"You think the SS would do such a test?"

"Of course they would. Remember, I was trained by the Waffen SS at the *Junkerschule* in Bad Tölz but I was a bit too short for promotion. There was also the small point about my Jewish grandparents, but today I am just an ordinary English waiter."

Claudia smiled at Werner.

"There is nothing ordinary about you, Werner."

"Thank you, my dear. Without a test, you see no one would believe it. They are German SS after all."

"So they would test him in a public setting?"

"Man muss es gesehen haben, um es zu glauben. In English, we say: You have to see it, to believe it. They are very practical people, the SS."

"Good point, Werner. I will talk to Paul. What's this nonsense about the RAF recruiting Luftwaffe pilots?"

"A joke, Claudia. Just a joke. You think I go too far?"

Martin joined in a laugh with Werner.

"Werner is a joker, Claudia. He likes to have fun with the Nazi bastard."

"I don't mind, Werner. Paul wants you to be yourself when you are with him. Be careful, though."

It was very late at night, but the powerful binoculars gathered enough light for Marek to make out the shapes of the Scots Guards inside the perimeter of the Mytchett house grounds. The men were standing around smoking and didn't appear very alert.

Marek, in his Polish military uniform, was lying behind a tree training his binoculars on the house when he noticed the second-floor window shade going up and the figure of a man backlit by a desk lamp. He didn't hesitate. He grabbed his

Mosin–Nagant scoped sniper rifle and quickly took aim at the man in the window. It was an easy shot for Marek at 350 yards. He got into a comfortable prone position and checked for wind drift. He took a deep breath, exhaling slowly with his finger on the trigger.

The Nazi *Reichsminister* suddenly let the drapes drop, killing the light from the room. Marek cursed under his breath. Through the scope, he saw a rim of light showing around the window, but the target was gone.

"I am happy to see that your leg has healed, Herr Hess," Major Foley said, sitting near the coffee table in the drawing room with Captain Cummings.

"It is still a bit stiff, sir," Z replied, clutching a mysterious box to his chest. "I can walk, but I can't run."

Claudia brought in a tea tray and put the pot and cups on the table for the meeting. She replaced the ashtray and left the room.

"Well, I am sure it will improve. I wanted to come down here and give you the news myself. I am sorry to have to tell you this, but your father has passed away."

Z gave no visible sign of emotion.

"*Mein herzlichstes Beileid, Herr Hess.* My condolences and those of my government. Johann Fritz Hess died on October 9. It was reported in the German papers, sir."

"My condolences, sir," Cummings repeated.

"I have made some requests recently to have you moved to a new location, a quieter, more hospitable place perhaps," Foley said. "Would you like that, Herr Hess?"

Z seemed totally unmoved and even hostile to this suggestion. He opened the box in his arms and dumped the contents on the table: biscuits, ryvita, cocoa, sugar and various pills. Cummings rolled his eyes at Foley, who seemed unperturbed by the prisoner's behaviour.

"What is this, Herr Hess?"

"I have been collecting these things for analysis, sir. I think they contain secret poisons. I intend to take them back to Germany at the end of the war and have them analysed."

"And what kind of poison do you think they might contain?" asked Foley, playing along with Z's obsession. "Maybe something like cyanide. Fast working. You bite down on it and you die within seconds."

"No, sir."

"Maybe something slow and lethal, like small doses of mercury. You know Napoleon died of arsenic poisoning. Maybe we should taste it to see whether it is fast acting or slow. What do you think?"

Foley picked up a piece of ryvita and swallowed it as Z looked on in shock. Cummings grinned at the major, who popped a few of Dicks' placebo pills into his mouth.

"What about the sugar and cocoa, both are rationed these days, Herr Hess? They could contain some rare plant distillate, like curare from the Amazon, that incapacitates the nerves in seconds."

Foley put some sugar on his finger and licked it, then did the same for the cocoa. Z seemed to realise that the major was mocking him.

"Tastes sweet to me. Do you think it will be a slow or fast death, Herr Hess?"

Z said nothing and looked truly humbled.

"Herr Hess, isn't it about time that you gave up this childish game? You are a representative of the German Reich and our PM has given instructions to make you comfortable and look after you. If we wanted you dead, we would have hanged you at Pentonville Prison, as we do all Nazi spies."

Cummings noticed the brief flash of anger in Z's eyes.

"Before I am off, I think the Captain here has a small present for you."

Cummings pulled a shoe box from a canvas bag at his feet and handed it to Z.

Foley made the announcement: "A new pair of shoes for our distinguished guest, which the Captain and I bought this morning on the High Street. Size 9."

Z opened the box and looked at the new pair of shoes. Foley winked at Cummings as Z sat there in stunned silence.

"Dr Dicks knows nothing about our suspicions, sir," Captain Cummings said.

It was a sunny day as Major Foley, accompanied by Cummings, took his black labrador on a walk along a leafy road near Camp Z. The dog ran ahead of the two men.

"Dicks is convinced we have the real Hess under lock and key and our continued surveillance is to learn all the secrets we can from the man."

"What about the lieutenants, Malone and Jackson?"

"They know nothing. They were fascinated by our famous prisoner with his picture in the newsreels and in magazines, but it has begun to wear off with all the complaints and the long nights."

"What about your relationship with the man?"

"It's good, sir. I think he trusts me. He likes Claudia's cakes and Werner's jokes."

The dog trotted back to his master with a stick in its jaws. Foley took the stick and threw it. The dog tore off after it.

"We think the German agent may still be around," Foley said. "He is not transmitting, so he must be using another method to communicate with his control. We think it may be an intelligence-gathering operation. That's why he targeted your wife and may go after other members of the team, ergo the move to the new location."

"Claudia is very nervous since the break-in," Cummings said. "We have a police officer on the doorstep, but even that is not much to calm her. So we will be quite happy to leave the area."

"Good. We should have news about the move shortly."

The dog returned, and Foley threw the stick again.

"Our man is talking to the shadows again," Cummings said. "My people think this Herr Oberst is either his flight training instructor or an SS officer."

Foley nodded.

"Werner has a theory. He thinks that if the SS had a man like Z under their wing, they would want to test his effect on the public, show him off a bit to their superiors, and see whether he could pull it off."

"We could check Hess' public appearances over the months leading up to his flight," Foley said.

"Yes, sir. There may be one public appearance too many when the real Hess was tied up in Berlin or in Munich."

"So you think the SS may have put Hess on the stage at a party rally in the north of Germany with people like Heydrich or Dietrich to test his effect on the public?"

"Yes, I do."

"That sounds like a logical step for them. The only way to test an imposter is to show him in public. It would build confidence in their plan. Good idea. I will have our people look into it."

Twenty-seven

Berlin 1973

"Several days later, MI6 came back with a press report about Rudolf Hess appearing at an SS recruitment rally in Stettin in February '41 while the real Hess was with Hitler in Munich on the same date," Cummings said. "So we had our locus for Z in and around Stettin, but we still didn't have the training facility and the real identity of our imposter."

Terry listened quietly, absorbed by Cummings' story.

"In June 1942, we moved him to the new location. The War Office had insisted that Z be treated for his 'psychopathic personality' in an institution where British officers were actually undergoing regular medical treatment, but not a mental hospital to thwart any attempt to repatriate the man."

"You mean that if they put the man in a mental hospital, they would be obligated to repatriate?" Terry asked.

"Exactly. You catch on quick, Doctor," Cummings laughed. "Under the Geneva Convention, Britain was obliged to repatriate any prisoner of war who was found insane, so they chose a regular hospital instead of a 'mental' hospital. I reckon it was pretty typical of the warped minds at the Foreign Office. The new site was the Maindiff Court Hospital in Abergavenny,

Wales. To legitimize its use, they changed the name to 'POW Reception Centre', Maindiff Court."

England, June 1942

It was a sunny day as a military staff car drove along a two-lane road through the English countryside. Lt Malone drove with Captain Cummings in the front and Z in the back. For their security, they were followed at a distance by a second car with four Scots Guards inside. Around midday, the first car pulled off the road near a river.

Under a tree on the riverbank, Cummings, Malone and Z ate a sandwich lunch. The second car with the Scots Guards was parked off the road nearby. Z was a fast eater and was soon lying on his back on the grass with his eyes closed.

"So, Mr Hess, what do you think of our English countryside?" Malone asked as he finished his sandwich.

"It's very beautiful, Lieutenant, but I think Germany is far more beautiful."

"This is a pretty place, but I was never in Germany, so I can't compare," Malone said, turning to Cummings.

"I haven't seen much of Germany myself, Malone. I've been to Cologne and Berlin, but I don't know the south: Bavaria, the Black Forest, the Rhine river valley, and the east," Cummings replied.

Z sat up and looked at the river.

"In Berlin, you must have been to the Tiergarten, Captain, but have you seen Dresden and the *Frauenkirchen* church?"

Cummings shook his head.

"What about Munich and its *Englischer Garten*?

"No, I have never been to Munich. Major Foley knows it

well. He told me that the park was built by an Englishman, Sir Benjamin Thompson, who later became Count Rumford and was the Bavarian minister of war."

"An Englishman in Munich?" Z asked.

"Germany is certainly a beautiful country. Claudia never ceases to say so even after her family had to flee the country."

The men relaxed, watching the slow progression of the river.

A car sped past the Scots Guards who sat on the grass at the side of the road eating their lunch from their mess kits. The car went around a curve and pulled over five hundred yards away behind a small copse of trees. A photographer from London exited the car with a fancy twin-lens reflex camera and a wooden tripod. He climbed a stile into a cow pasture and headed towards the river.

After a while, he managed to close the distance with his target, the staff car carrying the famous Rudolf Hess. He set up the camera on the tripod and observed the action through a long lens. On the edge of the water, he could see two Scots Guards chatting on the grass with a third man invisible to the camera. He set the f-stop for bright sunshine and satisfied himself that the focus was close to the infinity mark. Then he peered again through the lens, but the men had left the frame and disappeared from view.

From the road, the photographer heard the unmistakable sound of two cars starting up and driving off. He quickly collected his equipment and raced back across the pasture, stepping in a cow patty as he made his way back to his car. At the stile, he carefully placed his tripod on the other side of the wall and climbed over.

As he emerged from the pasture onto a rutted track leading back to the road, he ran into a man in a Polish military uniform carrying a long cardboard box.

"Sir, are you a journalist?" Marek asked.

The photographer walked away with the tripod on his shoulder, ignoring the impertinent Pole.

"Who do you work for, sir? Which paper? Maybe I can help you?"

The photographer hurried off walking quickly until suddenly he collapsed in the mud as a rock smashed his skull.

Twenty-eight

Abergavenny 1942

The Maindiff Court Hospital looked like a very large country house surrounded by trees. The staff car pulled up to the entrance, where a line of domestic staff waited to welcome the new arrival. Captain Cummings opened the door for Z, who stepped out cautiously in his Luftwaffe uniform, astonished by the reception committee. A line of hospital workers stood near the front steps to welcome the famous Nazi *Reichsminister*. Z shook hands with several doctors and nurses before the captain could pull him free to enter the building.

In the prisoner's wing, Cummings and Z walked around a suite of rooms on the ground floor with a verandah overlooking a small, wire mesh enclosed garden. There was a bedroom and a living room leading to the verandah. Z looked happily surprised by his new surroundings as Malone arrived with his baggage.

"Well, this is nice. What do you think?" Malone asked.

"Yes, it is a big improvement," Z replied.

Malone turned to Cummings.

"By the way, I met Colonel Davies of the Mardy POW camp down the road, sir. He invited us over for a drink once we get settled."

"Well, that's very nice of him," Cummings said.

"They just started to receive prisoners and already they are planning another camp across town. It is mainly U-boat and Luftwaffe men, not many officers."

Z listened with interest to Malone's comments.

"I have had a chat with the staff here," Cummings said. "We talked about your meals and the security arrangements."

"Are you worried that I will escape, Captain?" Z asked.

"Not really. The security is light but clearly present if you look around. This used to be a mental hospital, but now it is a military hospital. Down the hall, they look after the Dunkirk wounded, and it is not a pretty sight. How about a walk on Sugar Loaf Mountain tomorrow, sir?"

"I would like that, Captain."

"In Welsh, they call it Mynydd Pen-y-Fal."

"We would call it *Zuckerbrot Gebirge*."

"*Zuckerbrot*. The Sugar Loaf? Good."

The men looked up to see a new arrival in a Scots Guards uniform standing in the doorway.

"Hello, sir. I am Lt May."

May saluted the captain.

"I am Captain Cummings, and this is Lieutenant Malone. So you have come from Mytchett to join us?"

"Yes, sir. Here are my orders."

May handed Cummings a letter from his superior officer and the two men shook hands.

"Welcome to Wales, Lt May."

A train pulled into the Abergavenny train station, and Captain Cummings advanced along the crowded platform as numerous young soldiers disembarked. Steffi jumped down onto the platform and ran towards her dad, pulling on her mother's arm. Claudia let her go as she struggled with two very large suitcases.

"Hello, Daddy."

Steffi kissed her dad, who lifted her in his arms as he embraced Claudia.

"We missed you," Claudia said. "Steffi loves the farm in Dorset. It's quite primitive there, but mama and papa seem to like it."

Cummings took the bags from Claudia, and they walked along the platform to the exit.

"Papa has hens and a milk cow, Daddy. You know how many eggs I collected?"

"No, I wouldn't know, *Schatzi*."

"Veronika got four, and I got six, but I dropped one."

"Well, you must have had a nice time."

"I got a present for you, Dad. Guess what it is."

Cummings exchanged a look with Claudia, who smiled mysteriously at him.

"Animal, vegetable or mineral?" Cummings asked.

Steffi pulled a brown egg with coloured markings from her basket and showed it to her dad.

"It's an egg. Mum sucked out the yoke and then I coloured it for you. It's a decoration."

"It's beautiful. Thank you, *Schatzi*."

"Dad, I will keep it for you in the basket. Mum said it will get crushed if we put it in our pocket."

"Your mum is always right."

Cummings grinned at Claudia, amused by his daughter.

A staff car pulled up outside an old terraced Victorian red-brick house with a slate roof. Cummings and his family disembarked and headed towards the house while the driver collected their bags. Steffi ran through the front door ahead of her parents with a shriek of joy. Cummings and Claudia followed the child into their new home.

It was a warm summer night as Cummings lit a fire in the fireplace after Steffi had been put to bed. He sat with Claudia on the living room couch in the dark, looking at the red glow of the fire.

"I like the house," Claudia said. "It's quite cozy here and there's no leaky roof."

"It is nice, isn't it?"

"I like the garden. Steffi can play with her friends and we might be able to grow some vegetables back there, Paul."

"Wonderful. The neighbours seem nice enough."

"While you were out, the lady next door brought me a jar of homemade chutney and a young girl living across the way came by with a bowl of raspberries. Steffi ate most of them, I'm afraid."

Cummings picked up his glass of whisky.

"Wales is very friendly compared to London," Cummings said.

"Yes, it is. So how did it go with Z?"

"The hospital here is a great improvement over Mytchett and the staff are nice. You should have seen them lining up to shake his hand."

"They haven't had to live under the bloody Nazis, so they see him as some kind of celebrity," Claudia replied.

"Well, it makes our job easier."

"Yes, it does."

"I think we need to let him get settled and then make our move," Cummings said.

"You know he likes you, Paul. It won't be long before he spills the beans."

"Spills the beans?"

"You know that is my papa's favourite English expression. He says it comes from the Greeks. A white bean was a vote for a motion and a black bean was a vote against it. Then someone might spill the beans, annulling the vote."

"Z better spill the beans soon because we are running out of time, Claudia. People in London are getting impatient."

Twenty-nine

It was getting late as Lt Malone put down a Sam Spade novel and turned off the bedside lamp in the guardroom. It had been a long day on the road and he was exhausted. Just as he closed his eyes and prepared to go to sleep, Lt May stumbled into the room in the dark. He sat down on the bed opposite Malone's and took off his shoes.

"Hey Malone, I heard the crazy nutter tried to commit suicide."

"Where'd you hear that?" Malone asked.

"Come on, everyone was talking about it at Mytchett."

"Well, it's true, but Cummings says we aren't to talk about it. Better keep your mouth shut. Official secrets are no joking matter."

"You're Canadian, right?"

"Yes, I am. I came over in '38 hoping for a bit of action and signed up, but it's been mainly guard duty."

"Bloody awful boring work, Malone. I know it well. I've been doing guard duty at POW camps, ports, sensitive sites, the lot."

"I heard you say to the captain that you volunteered for the work here."

"Yeah, I reckon. Anything to get away from Camp Z. You

lock up the old bastard at night?"

"Yeah, but we no longer share his lodgings as we did at Mytchett. He was constantly waking us up at night."

"What's the captain like?"

"Nice chap, fair, keeps to himself. He's got a German wife and kid."

"That's bloody amazing."

"Better get some sleep, May. We'll be up early."

Captain Cummings in his Scots Guards' uniform and Z, wearing a flat cap and red scarf, walked along a heather and bracken-clad path to the top of the bald hill known as Sugar Loaf Mountain followed by two Maindiff orderlies. Located north-west of Abergavenny, it was the southernmost peak of the Black Mountains, with a height of some 600 metres.

They stopped to marvel at the view, looking north to the Black Mountains, east to the Cotswolds, west to the Brecon Beacons, and south to the Bristol Channel.

"This is not really a mountain, Captain," Z said. "It is more like a large hill?"

"Yes, you're right, sir. There aren't any high mountains in Wales, I'm afraid."

"You know we have the Zugspitze in Germany. It is a real mountain. It is almost 3,000 metres high, I think. Then in the Alps, we have the Matterhorn and the Mont Blanc at over 4,000 metres. No, this is just a small hill, Captain, but the view is very nice."

"Yes, it is. We better start down before it rains."

At the Cummings house, it was Steffi's birthday party. She

was four years old and sat in a new dress in front of a white angel cake sporting four candles. Opposite her sat Veronika, now a gangly ten years old and two young children from the neighbourhood. Paul, Claudia and her parents Markus and Rosa, Malone and Z sang happy birthday to young Steffi, who then blew out the candles with the help of her dad.

Claudia served the cake to the children and their guests. Suddenly there was a squeal of delight from Steffi at the sight of her birthday present, a large teddy bear with a red ribbon. Later that evening, the children played croquet in the yard. Malone helped Steffi slam a red ball through a hoop watched closely by Veronika while Z assisted another child with her ball. Cummings sat in a lawn chair nearby in the company of Rosa and Markus. Claudia brought over a tray of food.

"I never would have thought it possible to see our lovely Veronika playing croquet with a Nazi *Reichsminister* and a Scots Guardsman," Markus said.

Cummings and Claudia shared a laugh with Markus, as Rosa looked ill at ease.

"Please, Markus. He is Paul's guest."

"Yes, it is quite remarkable, Markus," Cummings said. "Who could ever have imagined it?"

"There is some very bad news coming out of Poland, Paul."

"What are you hearing?"

"Our friends in Vienna say that the SS are murdering Jews."

Markus had ties to several international efforts to save the Jews and was growing increasingly frustrated with the apathy toward the Jewish plight across Europe. Claudia sat down next to her dad.

"Who is saying this, Papa?"

"Markus got a call from our Jewish relief group," Rosa said. "Rabbi Solomon had it from his friends in Austria."

"It is crazy. They are slaughtering Jews across Poland and the Baltic States, Paul. They are using mobile gas chambers when they aren't shooting them."

"I am hearing similar things through our people. I don't know what our government can do, Markus."

"Let's not talk about it in front of the children, please," Rosa said as Claudia nodded in agreement.

Veronika was making a mess of her croquet game. Her ball was in an impossible position, so she turned to Markus for help.

"Papa, can you help me? I don't know what to do."

Markus got up to help Veronika while Rosa collected the food tray. She stopped near Claudia.

"Vero started calling him Papa this and Papa that just last week."

"I noticed. Well, I'm sure he doesn't mind. He was always a softie."

Rosa smiled at this comment.

"He loves being a dad again," Rosa said as she left for the kitchen with the tray.

Claudia watched her dad play croquet with Veronika. Malone and Steffi were way ahead on the course, but the neighbour's kids were gaining ground quickly with Z's help.

"I think he is ready to give it all up," Claudia said to her husband.

Paul watched Z, who was totally immersed in the game and having fun helping the children slam the ball through the hoops.

"*Ein Junge in einem Männerkörper.* He's a child in a man's body."

"I am not so sure," Paul replied.

"The man is a hopeless romantic, Paul. He is dying to tell

you the story of his life."

"You may be right, darling."

In the Maindiff prisoner's wing, Lt Malone was lying in bed reading a Raymond Chandler novel when Lt May stumbled into the room quite drunk.

"So how'd it go with the birthday party?"

"Had a great time. The kids loved it and so did Z."

"I can't believe the captain allowed that man to go to his kid's birthday party. That bloke is a fuckin' Nazi war criminal."

"The captain wants to keep him happy."

"Happy? Don't be daft. He's a bloody Nazi. He should be locked up or hanged by the neck."

"You should've seen him playing croquet. He loves kids, so perhaps he isn't all that bad," Malone said, barely lifting his eyes from his novel.

"I think he's a nutter, Malone. That's what I think. He's a danger to all of us."

Malone sighed and returned to reading about Detective Philip Marlowe.

Thirty

"Look old chap, I think it is about time we had a real talk," Cummings said as he followed Z in his flat cap and red scarf up the path through the heather and bracken to the top of Sugar Loaf Mountain.

"But we talk every day, Captain," Z replied.

"A real talk. No more lies."

Z stopped in his tracks and turned towards Cummings.

"*Was ist los?* What is wrong, Captain?"

They had arrived at the flat top of the hill, followed at a distance by two Maindiff orderlies.

"It is clear to me," Cummings said, looking at the superb view of the surrounding hills, "that you are not Rudolf Hess but a decoy sent to this country. We know a good deal about your past and it is not very distinguished. It has nothing to do with the famous Nazi *Reichsminister*."

Cummings glanced at Z and saw that he was having trouble breathing and had gone very pale.

"Are you all right, sir?" Cummings asked.

Cummings was reaching for his arm when Z suddenly collapsed. He curled up on the ground, writhing in pain.

"Is it your heart, old chap? Are you having an attack?"

Z looked back at Cummings and whispered.

"Ein Panikanfall. Einen Moment, bitte. It's a panic attack. Just a moment."

Z remained still with his eyes closed as Cummings looked on with apprehension. The Maindiff orderlies ran up to help the captain, but he signalled for them to keep their distance.

Near the base of the mountain, a car pulled into the car park. The driver remained at the wheel, looking up at the mountain. He picked up a pair of field glasses on the seat and searched for the captain and his charge on the mountain. He quickly identified Cummings and the two hospital orderlies, but their Nazi prisoner was no longer visible from below.

He stepped out of the car, removed his black fedora, and tossed it into the car. Marek grabbed the twin-lens reflex camera from the passenger seat and went to the boot to collect the wooden tripod. He crossed the road and headed up the path to the mountain.

Z had recovered from the panic attack. He stood up, and the captain handed him his cap. They started down the path together, with Z leaning on the captain's arm.

"Are you feeling better?"

"Yes, I am better. Thank you, Captain."

Z walked on silently.

"I think it is time for you to unburden yourself, to tell me the truth. Let me start by admitting a truth of my own. I am not a captain in the Scots Guards, but a case officer with our intelligence services."

Z looked stunned. He stopped walking and faced Cummings.

"You have been under surveillance for over a year now."

Z looked suddenly vulnerable, even frightened.

"Claudia and Werner never worked at Trent Park. That was their cover story to gain your trust. They work for our intelligence services. Of course, Dr Dicks and the Scots Guards know nothing about our work. The doctor knows about our surveillance, but has no idea as to your real identity."

"You are a spy. You have been spying on me?"

"Yes, absolutely. We would be negligent in our duty if we weren't keeping a close eye on you. You are an enemy agent, after all."

Cummings smiled at Z and grew wistful as he admired the view of the Black Mountains.

"You know this is quite an extraordinary view for Wales," Cummings said, "but not quite the view from the Berghof in the Obersalzberg. The Führer has a far better view, I think. Neville Chamberlain visited Hitler at the Berghof in '38. He was very impressed with the mountains but not so impressed by *Der Gefreite* ('the Corporal' referring to Hitler) I'm afraid."

"Are you going to send me back to Germany?"

"Certainly not while the war is on. The government has no plans to send you back," Cummings said, "so you don't have to worry. Your SS handlers would certainly have you disappear within a week."

Z looked stunned.

"You are out of the war now, just like any other German POW. You know these young men write letters to their family and all they talk about is what they want to do at the end of the war. What do you want to do at the end of the war?"

"I am not sure, Captain. I haven't thought about it."

"With the Americans on our side and the Russians fighting on your Eastern front, it is going to happen sooner or later.

What about your family in Germany? Your mother, Frieda, your brothers and sisters?"

Z was stunned to hear the captain use his mother's name.

"You must want to know what happened to them. I can find out for you."

"My family is dead," Z moaned.

"How do you know that?"

"I know it. I have seen the house. All the houses were destroyed. A man told me that the families had been removed."

"I am sorry to hear that."

"*Juden, sagte der Mann*. He called them Jews."

"Where is your home?"

"I cannot say."

"Look, old chap. We know you lived near Stettin. It is no longer a secret."

Z was astonished by the captain's knowledge.

"I can't help you if you give us nothing. Do you have a brother or a sister?"

"Yes, a younger brother."

"What's his name?"

Z hesitated for a long moment.

"Dieter."

"So you have no idea what happened to your mother, Frieda, and your brother, Dieter?"

"I have had no news. They were to be protected, they promised," Z complained.

"Who promised? Oh, that's right, we know who they are, don't we? Who is Herr Oberst?"

"They will kill me if I tell you."

"I think the SS sent your family away so they could better control you. Isn't that right?"

Z nodded and looked around nervously. The Maindiff orderlies watched him from a distance.

"I will look into it for you. We have the means to do it. *Wie heißen Sie?* What is your name?"

Z walked on, ignoring the question.

"*Ihr Name, bitte?*" Cummings persisted.

Z turned and looked at Cummings, finally relenting.

"*Max. Max Hörner. Meine Mutter ist Frieda Gunther.*"

"*Der Vater?* Your father?"

"Oskar Hörner, he died in the Great War."

"*Die Stadt?* The name of the town, please?"

"Malburg."

"Well, that is a good start, old chap. It's a pleasure to get to know you, Max Hörner."

On the steep path, Marek set up his camera with a long lens. He leaned over to look into the viewfinder and ground glass. He could see a closely framed image of Cummings and Z over a hazy background. He stepped back to gaze at the mountain with a self-satisfied smirk.

As the captain and Z descended the mountain, Marek quickly packed up his camera and tripod and hurried back to the car park.

Thirty-one

Captain Cummings typed a report on an old Underwood typewriter in the Maindiff office while Lt May smoked and read a newspaper at the front desk. Lt Malone entered the smoke-filled room with the morning mail.

"Damn it, May. Put that cigarette out, will you? This is a hospital, not a pub."

Malone turned to the captain.

"Here's your mail, sir."

Malone handed a telegram to Cummings, who tore it open.

"I reckon you should read it and tell me what you think," Cummings said to Claudia.

He was sitting on the sofa in the living room in the early evening. Steffi had gone to bed. Claudia poured the ersatz coffee into cups on the table and then picked up the telegram as Paul watched her.

"CONGRATS ON THE IDENTITY OF OUR MAN. VERY GOOD WORK. NEED YOU BACK IN LONDON. TIME IS RUNNING OUT. PLEASE ACCELERATE SOFT APPROACH. UNDER GREAT PRESSURE TO BRING

YOUR MAN BACK TO LONDON. MAJOR FOLEY.

"The message is perfectly clear, Paul. The major wants you back in London as soon as possible."

"I agree. That part is clear, but what do you make of the second part, Claudia?" asked Cummings. "Accelerate soft approach? Bring your man back to London?"

"You have given them a name, Paul. Now they want the whole shebang."

"But they have known Z was an imposter for over a year," Cummings said. "Why the rush now?"

"Because they have his real name, Paul. They can treat Max Hörner like any other POW."

Cummings stood up and walked around the room with growing frustration.

"What are they going to do to the man?" Cummings said. "Put him through the usual sleep deprivation, beatings, cold water treatment and then throw him into a POW camp."

"I doubt they will get anything with their methods. He will just clam up," Claudia replied.

"We are starting to get results."

"We've seen it all before, Paul," Claudia said. "I don't want to return to London. Steffi is just getting used to life here in Wales. I don't know what we can do."

"They will put Z back in a cell at Latchmere House and after a time he will end up in a POW camp," Cummings said. "And we will return to babysitting German agents."

"It certainly looks that way, *Liebling*."

In the prisoner's quarters, Z ate powdered eggs with toast and drank tea from a breakfast tray. Nearby, Lt May was writing notes in his journal just as Bronwen, a rather plain girl in kitchen whites with rosy cheeks, entered the room.

"Everything fine, sir?"

"*Das schmeckt gut.* The eggs taste good. The paprika improves the taste."

Bronwen looked happily at the famous German prisoner.

"You are a good cook, *Fräulein*. What is your name?"

"Bronwen, sir."

"How old are you, Bronwen?"

"35 years this year, sir."

"You look much younger, I think."

Bronwen smiled at Z, who seemed to have taken a shine to the young woman.

"So, your family lives nearby?"

"Llanarth, sir. It is a small village."

"Do you have brothers and sisters?"

"Yes, sir. My two brothers are in the war with the Royal Welsh. My sisters work the farm with my mam. Dad, he can't work 'cause he is in a wheelchair."

"What happened to your dad?"

"The great war, sir. A shrapnel wound."

"*Es tut mir Leid.* I am sorry."

"Anything else, sir?"

"More toast, please."

As Bronwen returned to the kitchen to fetch the toast, Z looked daggers at Lt May.

"Lt May, where's my toast? I had two slices."

"You gave me a slice, sir," May replied.

"No, I didn't. I would remember if I did."

"But, sir, you asked me to take one."

"I don't remember giving you anything."

May raised an eyebrow, put his journal away, and picked

up the newspaper.

After a late evening meal at home, Cummings sang *Hoppe Hoppe Reiter* (Bumpety Bump Rider) to Steffi, sitting on his knee, accompanied by Claudia. Nearby, Z watched the happy couple.

> *"Hoppe hoppe Reiter*
> *wenn er fällt, dann schreit er,*
> *fällt er in den Teich,*
> *find't ihn keiner gleich.*
>
> *fällt er in den Graben,*
> *fressen ihn die Raben.*
>
> *fällt er in den Sumpf,*
> *dann macht der Reiter plumps!"*

> (Bumpety bump, rider,
> if he falls, then he cries out.
> Should he fall into the pond,
> no one will find him soon.
>
> Should he fall into the ditch,
> then the ravens will eat him.
>
> Should he fall into the swamp,
> then the rider goes splash!)

"Plumps! (Splash)" laughed Steffi as Cummings tipped her on the floor.

"*Noch einmal. A*gain, Daddy."

"That's enough. Time for bed. *Gib Papa einen Kuss*," Claudia said.

Cummings kissed the child.

"OK, *Schatzi*. Bedtime."

Claudia collected Steffi and turned to Z, who was sitting nearby drinking whisky.

"Say goodnight to Mr Hess."

"Good night."

"In German, please," Claudia insisted.

"*Gute Nacht, Herr Hess.*"

"*Gute Nacht*," Z replied.

Claudia left the room with Steffi as Cummings went over to the drinks table to pour himself another whisky.

"Max, don't you want to go home?"

"*Nach Hause, nein.*"

"Do you want to stay in England?"

"Yes, I would like that."

"Find a job, build a life here?"

"I like Wales. The people are very nice here."

Claudia returned from the bedroom.

"You need to find a woman, Max, get married and found a family," said Claudia.

Z nodded silently.

"Did they tell you what happened to the real Rudolf Hess after you left?" Cummings asked.

"No."

"We think they killed him, Max. It has been over a year now and he still hasn't surfaced."

"You think they killed him?" Z asked.

"Of course. What do you think?"

"I don't know. Maybe they are keeping him hidden until I

return."

"What about yourself, Max?" Claudia asked. "When were they going to pull you out?"

"Pull me out?"

"*Zurückholen*. We call it extraction, Max," Cummings said. "You are way past your sell-by date, old chap, if I may say so."

"They never talked about extraction. They said I was to come to talk about peace."

"Didn't you wonder how you would get home, Max? I certainly would have," Claudia said.

"Yes, I wondered. I thought the British government would send me back."

"So, how were you to contact your control? Your letters to Ilse? Is Ilse your contact?" Claudia inquired with a furtive glance at her husband.

Z remained silent.

"Come on Max. You are with friends. We know about Ilse, Karl Haushofer, Frau Rothacker and Professor Gerl. All your correspondence is read," Cummings said.

Claudia attempted a more artful approach.

"You are quite poetic in your letters, Max. You talk about the red earth, the distant mountain changing colour. Ilse knows you are in Wales. Is she your contact?"

"Or is it Professor Gerl? He was the Hess family doctor in the Allgau, wasn't he? Does he work for the SS?"

Z shook his head.

"What were your instructions about aborting the mission once you got to Britain?" Cummings asked.

"There were no abort instructions, Captain."

Z cracked his knuckles nervously.

"They said that if I revealed my identity or confessed, they would find me and kill me."

162

"Were they going to send in a team, Max?" Claudia asked with a serious air.

"Yes, they would come for me."

"How were they to do this?" Cummings asked.

"They would use a commando. They have men in the POW camps who could do the job."

Cummings and Claudia glanced at each other in bemused disbelief as Z finished his drink.

Thirty-two

Captain Cummings and Z sat on the top of a wall looking across at White Castle, a medieval castle built in the 13th century near Abergavenny. Z drew the walls and the towers of the main defences on a sketchpad with a pencil. Lt May, holding a Sten submachine gun, provided security a hundred yards away.

Z showed the drawing to the captain, who was impressed by its realistic quality.

"You're an artist, Max. Lovely drawing."

"Thank you."

"Where did you learn to draw?"

"I was always drawing as a young boy, Captain."

Z looked up after touching up an area on the sketch with his pencil.

"I would draw in the margin of my notebooks, sketch faces and landscapes. My teachers were always complaining that I wasn't paying attention."

"Well, you certainly have a gift for it. By the way, Max, I inherited two greyhounds recently from some chums of mine. You know *Windhunde*."

"*Windhunde*, they are wonderful dogs, Captain."

"These dogs race every Saturday over at the Merthyr Tydfil

dog track, Max."

"Racing dogs?"

"Yes, Malone is bringing them up so you can have a look."

As Cummings and Z made their descent from the castle, they ran into Lt Malone with the greyhounds on leashes, coming up their way.

"Aren't they beautiful animals, Max?"

Z petted the first dog, which soon went wild, jumping up and down.

"*Guter Hund, braver Hund. Bei Fuß.* Good dog, heel boy. What is his name?"

"This is Nimrod, that one is Noah. You like dogs, Mr Hess?" Malone asked.

"Yes, I love dogs."

"I have to walk them every day. They need the exercise," Malone said.

"I'd like to come out with you one day, Lieutenant."

"Please do, sir."

Malone pulled the two dogs away and headed up towards the castle.

Captain Cummings and Z walked down to the car park, followed at a distance by Lt May. On the way down, the lieutenant slipped something into a copy of the *Western Mail* newspaper and dumped it in a bin in the car park before joining Cummings and Z at the staff car. May got behind the wheel next to Cummings, with Z in the back, and drove away.

A short time later, a car pulled up and a man in a dark trench coat rifled through the refuse in the bin, removing the copy of the *Western Mail*.

In the enclosed garden behind the Maindiff Hospital, Z collected wild blackberries near the back wall. He looked over and noticed Veronika leading Steffi on a pony around the field next door.

"Hello, Veronika. That is a nice pony."

"Steffi is riding a pony for the first time, sir."

"Do you like ponies, Steffi?"

"I love them. Everyone does."

"Not everyone, my dear. Some people prefer noisy machines like trains, automobiles, and airplanes."

"Not me," shrieked Steffi as the pony broke into a trot, running after Veronika holding the reins.

"Where is your mama, dear?"

"She is with Lt Malone," Veronika said. "She is bringing you something sweet to eat."

Malone called to Z from the verandah.

"Claudia is here, sir. If you like, we can go for a walk later."

"Can we go with the dogs, Lieutenant?" Z asked from the garden.

"Of course, we can take the dogs."

Z's face lit up as he climbed the steps to the verandah.

"Do you have enough reading materials, Herr Hess?" Claudia asked.

"Yes, I am good," Z replied.

Claudia and Z were taking their tea on the verandah. Dressed in her WAAC uniform, Claudia watched Z devour a piece of *Apfelstrudel*. She looked around to see whether Malone was in the vicinity.

"I think it is better that we continue with your official

identity. Don't you think, Max?"

"Yes, of course."

"Would you like to read some plays by Shakespeare, Herr Hess? I can bring them."

"Yes, I would like that."

Claudia smiled as Z ate another piece of *Apfelstrudel*.

"Do you know Goethe's *Das Göttliche*, Claudia? In English they call it 'The Divine'."

Claudia nodded as Z recited the words from memory.

"Edel sei der Mensch, Hilfreich und gut!
Denn das allein, Unterscheidet ihn,
Von allen Wesen, Die wir kennen."

(Let man be noble, generous and good!
For that alone distinguishes him
From all the living beings we know.)

Claudia repeated the final line along with Z.

"I learned it at school. It is a beautiful poem. You enjoy reading Goethe?"

"It is my greatest pleasure."

"Those are lovely sentiments from another time, but even you must admit that the reality of life in Germany today is very different. The Nazis have turned Germany into a living hell."

"*Nein, Frau Claudia*. It is not the fault of the National Socialist Party. Our intentions were always pure. It is the war that brought this on, and men like Bormann. The Führer never wanted this."

"Goethe is all about man's best intentions," Claudia said. "Hitler is all about man's basest, most ignoble intentions. He is a criminal."

"The Führer is a wonderful man, *Frau Claudia!*" Z protested. "He does not want war with Britain. I came here to deliver a message of peace to the British government, but they have refused to enter into a negotiation."

Claudia raised her eyebrows in silent fury. She finished her tea and stood up.

"*Auf wiedersehen, Herr Hess.* I must be going. I will look for more reading material for you."

Claudia retreated from the room as young Bronwen entered to collect the tea tray.

"*Fräulein Bronwen,* how are you today?"

"I am fine, Mr Hess."

"Have some *Apfelstrudel.* The captain's wife brought it."

"Oh, I couldn't, sir. It does look very good."

"If you don't eat a piece, then Lt Malone or Lt May will eat the rest, please."

"Well, just a small piece, then."

Bronwen took a piece of *Apfelstrudel,* savouring the sourness of the tart apples and the sugary sweetness of the pastry. She licked her fingers.

"It is divine, Herr Hess. I don't think I have ever eaten anything quite as good. I must ask Mrs Cummings for the recipe."

"Divine, yes. But not *göttlich,* I think," Z said with a sly grin.

Lt Malone and Z had just rounded a bend in the road on a long walk in the Brecon Beacon mountains when the greyhounds started barking. Lt May brought up the rear, carrying a Sten submachine gun. He raised the barrel when he saw a large open truck loaded with German POWs for the

Breconshire Camp stopped in the road ahead of them.

A small group of armed soldiers stood in the road near a military jeep watching the prisoners while a mechanic had the hood up and was tinkering with the spark plugs and distributor cap. One of the POWs glanced down from the truck, then did a double take and elbowed the man next to him as Malone and Z approached with the dogs, followed by a nervous Lt May holding the submachine gun.

"*Scheiße!*" the prisoner exclaimed. "*Das ist der Reichsminister Rudolf Hess.*"

"*Nazi-Arsch* (Nazi arsehole)."

The prisoners became agitated as one after another spotted Z's mug.

"Look at that! It's that Hess fella they talk about in the papers," a soldier said.

"Can't be. They would have hanged that arsehole by now," another said.

"That's him alright. I saw it in the paper last week. Bloody kraut. Go to hell."

The German POWs called out to one another as Lt Malone and Z passed by the truck followed by Lt May. Malone struggled to control the dogs and Z stared fixedly ahead, trying to ignore the barrage of shouts and muttered insults.

Marek climbed the outer wall at the back of the Maindiff Hospital. It was late at night, but even in the darkness, he had a perfect view looking down into Z's quarters through the enclosed garden. There was no sign of Hess, but Marek was a patient man. He silently removed his sniper rifle from his rucksack and assembled it. He then pointed the rifle at the verandah, searching for a target.

PLAYING RUDOLF HESS

Unbeknownst to Marek, Z was asleep on the couch and invisible to the visitor as Mozart's *Eine Kleine Nachtmusik* played quietly on the gramophone. As the music came to an end, Z woke up and started to move around the room.

Thirty-three

Colonel Davies was an old, rather pompous war-horse with a large waxed handlebar moustache, a pipe in his pocket and spit-shined shoes. Before the war, he had commanded a regiment of Gurkhas in India and returned to Britain with the evacuation of Dunkirk in May 1940. In the King's Head pub, Davies was carrying on with Lt Baker and several officers of the Mardy POW camp as Lt May entered and went to sit in a corner.

"Time to go, men. Good night to you, Toby."

The barman Toby nodded at Davies as he took a pint over to Lt May.

"Cheerio, you grumpy old git," said one officer to Toby on leaving. Toby gave him the two-finger salute as the men stumbled out the door, heading back to camp.

Colonel Davies and Lt Baker took the muddy shortcut back to the Mardy camp. They stumbled along the lane in the dark, making their way down towards the Gavenny River behind the Maindiff hospital. The two men stopped to take a piss in the bushes and observed silently Z's verandah across the field. Davies stopped moving.

"Lieutenant, have you got your gun?" Davies whispered.

Baker nodded and grasped his Webley service revolver.

"Come on, there's a peeping tom behind the hospital. We'll give him a good scare."

The two men headed across the muddy field towards the back of the Maindiff hospital.

Marek waited patiently for his target, poking his rifle through the wire grille. Z stood up and went over to the gramophone, just out of sight. The movement caught Marek off guard, but he quickly sighted his rifle on where Z's head had been and waited for him to return. It would be an easy kill shot.

All of a sudden, he was pulled backwards off the wall and found himself looking up at two men in uniform. The younger one was pointing a revolver at him as he snatched the rifle from his hands.

"Well, well. What have we got here?" Davies said. "I doubt he is a peeping tom?"

Marek weighed his chances. There were two of them, but the older one was unarmed and looked harmless.

"Sir, look at this," Baker said.

As Davies and Baker looked at the sophisticated firearm with stupefaction, Marek used the split second to pull a stiletto switchblade from his pants pocket and to lunge at Baker, slashing his forearm. Baker quickly stepped backwards, raising the sniper rifle as Marek in desperation, went for him again with the stiletto. Davies pulled a short kukri blade from his boot and with lightning speed jumped Marek, putting the Polish butcher in a chokehold.

"I wouldn't do that if I were you, dear boy. I might have to cut your throat."

As Marek looked at the famous curved blade inches away from his face, Baker gently removed the stiletto from his hand.

"A peeping tom, sir?"

"Not bloody likely. This fella is a professional assassin," Davies replied with a laugh. "Are you all right?"

"I think so," Baker said, lifting his arm as blood dripped all over his uniform.

"Give me your Webley, Lieutenant."

Baker handed the Webley to Davies, who relaxed his grip on the prisoner.

"We'll get you some first aid back at camp," Davies said. "Let's go."

Davies kicked Marek, who started walking with the Webley trained on his back, followed by Baker with the sniper rifle.

"Colonel, I didn't know an old-timer like you could move so fast."

"That wasn't very fast, Lieutenant," Davies laughed. "I am slower than I used to be. A Gurkha trained with a kukri can slit your throat in a fraction of a second."

The two men led their prisoner away.

Lt May finished his pint and left the pub. A man in a dark suit and trench coat stepped away from the bar and took his drink over to the corner table where May had been sitting. He sat down and, with his free hand, pulled out several sheets of notepaper stuck to the underside of the table. He quickly read the notes as he finished his drink.

Toby called to him as several customers left the pub.

"Last orders, sir. We're closing in 15."

"I'm fine, thanks," the man said.

"Sir, I am not sure I understand you correctly. You have arrested a peeping tom, and the man had a Russian sniper's rifle."

In the darkened hospital office, Lt Malone was standing next to the front desk, talking on the phone while he doodled on a scrap of paper.

"Yes, sir. I will call my superior officer."

Malone hung up and dialed Captain Cummings at home. He waited a moment as Cummings came on the line.

"Hello, sir. Sorry to call so late. There has been an incident here at Maindiff. Colonel Davies has arrested a peeping tom, a foreign chap with a gun."

"Quite the trophy, this peeping tom," Davies remarked, lighting his pipe. "Lt Baker had to have a few stitches in his arm after the bastard cut him with a switchblade."

Captain Cummings, Claudia and Lt Malone were sitting in Colonel Davies' office.

"We think that Claudia here may be able to recognize the man, Colonel," Cummings said.

"Let me show you his firearm, Captain."

Davies stood up to show his visitors the Mosin-Nagant sniper rifle lying on an adjoining desk.

"This is a model 91/30 according to my man Helmut," Davies said. "He knows it well since the Soviet sniper program was developed with the help of the Germans in the 1930s. This is quite a sophisticated piece of equipment and well maintained."

"I read that the Finnish sniper Simo Hayha used the same weapon during the Winter War against the Soviets," said

Malone.

"Yes, you're right, Lieutenant," Davies said. "I believe the Russians called him the 'White Death' after he killed over 500 of their men."

"You think he might be Russian?" Cummings asked.

"We don't know. He hasn't said a word, Captain. He's in the solitary cage. I will have an officer take you over there."

An officer led Cummings, Claudia and Malone through the gate into the POW camp surrounded by machine-gun posts and barbed wire. A few wolf whistles and catcalls were heard as the men admired Claudia in her WAAC uniform.

The officer summoned a young prisoner Helmut, who accompanied the group as they made their way towards a wire enclosure with a tin roof. Inside, a man wrapped in a blanket was sitting on a bench.

"*Stehen Sie bitte auf. S*tand up please," Helmut ordered.

The man on the bench turned his head briefly to smile at Claudia.

"*Stehen Sie auf.*"

"*Macht nichts,*" Cummings said, annoyed by the smirking prisoner. "It doesn't matter. Claudia, is he the man?"

Claudia nodded to her husband as Marek stood up.

"*Guten Tag, Fräulein.* Want some pork chops with the beef? Ha, ha. I am your Polish butcher. My name is Marek. Ha, ha."

"It's him, Paul. Let's go."

Marek grinned lewdly and laced his fingers through the wire mesh.

"Come back, miss. I'm just a butcher, a Polish butcher," Marek said as Cummings led Claudia away.

Thirty-four

London 1942

"Wie heißen Sie?" asked Stephens. *"Sprechen Sie Russisch oder Polnisch?"*

Handcuffed to a chair in the interrogation room at Latchmere House, Marek remained silent and refused to look at Lt-Colonel Stephens and Captain Short.

"You killed a butcher and were arrested for attempting to kill a German prisoner of war," said Stephens. "These are serious crimes. Who sent you?"

Marek remained immobile, ignoring the questions. Major Frank Foley and Captain Cummings watched the interrogation through the glass separation.

"All right, young man. We are giving you a choice. If you collaborate with our services, we might be able to prevent your hanging. If you don't collaborate, you will most certainly be hanged as a German spy."

Marek remained silent, ignoring Stephen's words.

"Get him out of my sight," Stephens ordered the two soldiers standing at the door. They quickly grabbed the prisoner and hauled him away.

In the observation room, Foley turned to Cummings.

"Stephens thinks our man may be NKVD. The rifle was Russian, and he had roubles in his pocket. Of course, it could be a good cover if he is working for the Germans. I am afraid it is going to take some time to break him."

"NKVD? I didn't know the NKVD was operating in Britain."

"We liaise with them through the embassy. They are thugs in any sense of the word. Stalin doesn't trust his closest allies."

Stephens and Short took a break and left the interrogation room.

"I ran the names in Malburg," Foley said. "Our people confirm that the village was destroyed by the SS in 1940. They think that the mother and son may be in a camp, maybe Sobibor or Treblinka."

"Very well, I will tell him. That's not the best of news."

"Before I go to 'C', I will need more. The flight trainer, the airbase, the SS unit, his orders, full disclosure. You know they may want to put him in a POW camp."

"I know, but he won't last a week in a POW camp."

Abergavenny 1942

Captain Cummings was at home watching Claudia bathe Steffi in the kitchen sink and then wrap her in a towel.

"Daddy, I'm learning to ride a bike," Steffi said with pride. "Lt Malone showed me."

"Let's just say that the lieutenant put Steffi on a child's trainer bike and gave her a little run around the Maindiff car park," Claudia said.

"Well, aren't you growing up fast, *Schatzi*"

Claudia helped Steffi into her pyjamas.

"Off you go now. Go find a book so your daddy can read to you," Claudia said as Steffi ran off to the bedroom.

"So Max may have to go to a POW camp?"

"It's possible. We really don't know at this point," Cummings replied.

"I will bring in a good German *Marmorkuchen* next week. That will raise his spirits. Does he know about Marek?"

"No, we have kept it from him."

"I'm glad they caught that man."

Steffi returned to the kitchen, holding up a book. Cummings lifted her up so she could kiss her mother.

"*Gib Mama einen Kuss, Schatzi.* Time for bed."

Claudia kissed Steffi and Cummings led her to her room for the bedtime story.

"Quite a lucky break for us," Colonel Davies said. "Most of our arrests are drunken yobs. None of them have Russian sniper rifles."

"Great work, Colonel."

Cummings glanced out the mess hall window at the prisoners milling about under the watchful eye of the soldiers manning a machine-gun post at the Mardy POW camp. He turned back just as Helmut arrived with a tray and Davies helped himself to another whisky.

"This is Helmut, one of our first prisoners."

"Yes, I've met Helmut."

"Say hello, Helmut. This is Captain Cummings."

Helmut nodded amiably at Cummings and retreated silently to the bar.

"Helmut was a U-boat engineer who kept the machines running until the day he was captured off the Irish coast. He has been very helpful here at the camp. He repaired our auxiliary power generator."

The colonel looked out the window at the POW camp as Lt Malone appeared with a drink at the captain's side.

"We have had a hard time getting this place up and running. Three months ago, there was nothing here. We had the prisoners in tents for the first few weeks, but now things are better."

"How many prisoners are you expecting, Colonel?"

"Not more than 400 without additional housing. They are trickling in every week now, mostly Kriegsmarine and Luftwaffe. White patches mainly, but now and then a black patch, mainly Waffen SS and paratroopers. We have to keep an eye on those chaps."

At the bar, Helmut turned up a BBC report on the radio. The announcer read the news:

"We are breaking programming to announce that Canadian forces and British commandos today attacked the German-occupied port of Dieppe and were strongly repulsed with major loss of life. It is estimated that some 3,000 men have been killed or taken prisoner. Reports say that Allied fire support was insufficient and the raiding party was trapped on the beach. We will have further news on the hour. Now, back to our music programming."

The radio played *There will be Bluebirds over the White Cliffs of Dover* by Vera Lynn as an air of extreme sadness invaded the room. Dieppe was turning out to be a major cockup for Allied forces.

Colonel Davies went over to the bar and whispered something to Helmut. He then turned to face the room, raising his hands for silence. He cleared his throat and stepped forward with a fierce look on his face.

"Let us take a moment to say a prayer for our Canadian and British comrades who died on the beach at Dieppe. We all know what that means after our defeat at Dunkirk. Please join us, Captain Cummings, for a minute of silent prayer."

The men lowered their heads and prayed silently while Vera Lynn sang her melancholy song in the background. At the bar, Helmut poured out ten shot glasses of whisky.

"You may have noticed that our barman Helmut is serving ten whiskies. The ten glasses are to honour our fallen comrades. They symbolize that our comrades are here with us in spirit."

Helmut solemnly finished pouring the whisky and put the bottle down quietly. He picked up the tray of drinks and brought it over to the colonel.

"You will notice that the glass is clear, like the purity of their hearts when answering the call of duty. The smoky taste is the salt spray from their landing craft. The amber colour is the sunshine on their youthful faces."

"They shall not grow old, as we will grow old. Age shall not weary them, nor the years condemn them. And death shall have no dominion."

Davies, with great pride, looked around the room at the tearful men who had all lost brothers and friends in the grinding tedium of the war.

"We will remember them as the sun goes down in the evening and as the sun comes up in the morning. We shall not forget the brave men who climbed the beaches at Dieppe. Let us never forget their sacrifice. To our fallen comrades!"

With one voice, the men said: "To our fallen comrades!"

Davies turned to Cummings.

"Please, Captain, it would be an honour to have you raise the first glass to the fallen."

Cummings looked at Malone.

"Lt Malone is Canadian, Colonel. Let him raise the first glass."

"Lt Malone, it would be an honour," Davies said with emotion.

Malone stepped up nervously. Davies handed him the first of the whisky shot glasses as the men waited their turn. Malone held up the drink solemnly.

"Slainte. To the Canadians!"

Malone drank the whisky.

"Now, Captain, it is your turn, sir."

Cummings picked up the second glass and held it up high for a moment.

"To the Canadians! To our Tommies who died on the beaches!"

Cummings polished off the whisky as Davies picked up the third shot glass and looked around at the men before downing it as the men spontaneously applauded. The men crowded around to collect a glass from the tray.

Malone turned to Cummings.

"I don't think we will be fit for any hard work this afternoon, sir."

"Don't worry, Malone. If these chaps hadn't caught Marek, our entire operation would have been compromised and we would be back in London, dodging bombs," Cummings said, feeling a bit maudlin after Davies' moving speech.

Thirty-five

Cummings stumbled into the kitchen as Claudia was preparing the evening meal. Little Steffi ran into his arms and he gave her a kiss before putting her down among the toys on the floor.

"How are you, *Liebling*?" Claudia asked.

Cummings looked a little unsteady on his feet and sat down heavily at the kitchen table.

"Are you all right?"

"I'm fine, darling," Cummings said. "I've just had a bit too much to drink, that's all."

"You don't look so fine."

"Well, I am sure there are others who are in far worse shape than I am. I left Malone at Maindiff and I had to help him up the stairs."

"Where have you been?" Claudia asked.

"We had a little ceremony over at the POW camp for the men who died at Dieppe. You must have heard about it on the radio?"

"Yes, Markus called. He thinks the British won't find the courage to liberate Europe after Dieppe."

"That's rather defeatist, don't you think?"

"Poor papa, he worries so."

"Colonel Davies put on quite a show. He's Welsh, you know. He has had an interesting career with the Gurkhas in India."

Claudia stirred the soup on the stove, watching her husband.

"It was all rather moving, you know," Cummings said and started to recite from memory: 'They shall not grow old, as we shall grow old. Age shall not weary them, nor the years condemn them. And death shall have no dominion'."

"Isn't that from the poet Dylan Thomas, *Liebling*? 'And death shall have no dominion'. I think it's a poem on immortality. I heard a reading of it on the radio."

"I knew I had heard the line somewhere. Davies must have borrowed it."

"It's about the human spirit and how we carry on after death. It's quite a wonderful poem. He has a lot in common with our German poets such as Rilke, Heine, and others, you know."

"Rilke? Do you remember *Das Stunden-Buch* (the Book of Hours)?" Cummings asked. "You read it to me in Cologne. It was quite wonderful."

"Of course, I do, *Liebling*."

"I still remember some of the lines," Cummings said as he recited from memory and was joined by Claudia.

"Lösch mir die Augen aus: ich kann dich sehn,
wirf mir die Ohren zu: ich kann dich hören,
und ohne Füße kann ich zu dir gehn,
und ohne Mund noch kann ich dich beschwören."

(Extinguish my sight, and I can still see you;
plug up my ears, and I can still hear you;

even without feet I can walk toward you,
and without mouth I can still implore you.)

Claudia fetched the bottle of whisky from the drinks table and poured two glasses.

"I think we need a drink, don't you, *Liebling*."

"Yes, I do. It's been a day for nostalgia, darling," Cummings smiled with a sorrowful look.

Claudia lifted her glass to make a toast.

"Here's to Rilke and Thomas," Claudia said.

"The only sane people in this dreary world," Cummings added.

"Cheers, my love. Cheers, *Liebling*."

"You know how it works?" Lt Malone asked.

Z looked bewildered.

"I have never seen a dog race."

"You will soon," Cummings smiled at Z, who was wearing his flat cap and sunglasses to hide his face.

The three of them were sitting in folding chairs on a Saturday evening near an oval track in the village of Merthyr Tydfil. Malone was a frequent visitor to the track and loved to race the greyhounds.

"The dogs chase a lure on the track until they cross the finish line," Malone said.

"A lure?" Z asked, watching the dogs going into their box on the track.

"You'll see soon enough," Cummings said.

Suddenly the bang of the starter gun was heard, and a cry went up from the spectators as the dogs took off after the lure. Cummings observed the lead dogs through his binoculars and then passed them along to Z to have a look.

"You see Nimrod in red, Noah is in blue," Cummings said.

On the first turn, Nimrod was in second place but was overtaken by Noah after the third turn, and then Nimrod overtook both Noah and the top dog in the final turn. Z was jumping up and down in excitement at seeing his dog win.

"*Das ist wunderbar*. Nimrod won the race. Incredible."

"Congratulations, sir. Nimrod's in his prime," Malone said. "He is only two years old, but he is very fast. He doesn't always want to win, so we are very lucky today. There are some very strong dogs in the race."

"A great run. I bet you never won on a dog in Germany, Herr Hess," Cummings said.

"Never, sir."

The men sat down and Cummings passed around a silver flask of whisky to celebrate the win as they watched the second race get started.

As Cummings and Z packed up the folding chairs and put them in the boot of the staff car, Malone went to collect the dogs from the track master and their winnings.

"You enjoy dog racing, Max?" Cummings asked.

"To watch those dogs run is a delight, Captain."

"I will be leaving shortly, moving back to London with Claudia and Steffi. I have given Noah to Malone, but I was thinking that maybe my old friend Max would like to have Nimrod. What do you say?"

"You are giving me the dog?"

"Why not? You can walk him every day. Malone keeps the dogs at the kennel."

"It would be an honour to own such a *Windhund*."

"Well, then you must have him."

After leaving the dogs at the kennel with Lt Malone, Cummings drove Z back to the Maindiff Hospital. They climbed out of the car and headed up the front steps to the hospital.

"I want you to meet a friend of mine," Cummings said to Z as they entered the building.

Instead of entering Z's private wing of the hospital, they stepped into the military wing of the hospital, which cared for wounded soldiers. Numerous beds lined the corridors and the stink of bedpans was omnipresent. Z had never been in this part of the hospital and was surprised by the number of injured soldiers.

A nurse recognized Cummings and let him pass with his visitor. They entered a large ward with beds equipped with Murphy drips occupied by the severely wounded. It was a light airy place with the afternoon sun in the windows. They approached the bed of Cummings' injured friend.

"Max, meet Desmond. Des is an old school chum of mine."

Desmond was a young man, missing a sizeable chunk of his face and skull. Wrapped in gauze, his only visible eye winked at them as Cummings squeezed his hand.

"Hello, Des. How are you feeling?"

Desmond's eye winked at them.

"Des, this is my friend Max. Des was wounded at Dieppe when a mortar hit his landing craft. He arrived last week."

Z felt very uncomfortable, but couldn't take his eyes off the young man.

"I have been coming in here to help keep up the men's morale. Sometimes I play a hand of cards with his pals over there. This is where we keep our worst cases, Max. We hide them away in places like Maindiff."

Z looked around at the other beds. All the men were in a terrible state, with lost limbs and terrible head wounds. Many were drugged to the gills and there was a nasty smell of suppurating wounds.

"Let's have a drink with Des," Cummings said, smiling at the injured man. "You don't mind, do you, old boy?"

Cummings removed the silver flask from his pocket and poured a drink for Z in a glass on the bedside table. He handed the glass to Z and took a swig directly from the flask himself.

"*Prost*, Captain."

"Cheers, Max."

Cummings pointed to his ears.

"Des can't hear us. I thought you might like to meet your neighbours."

Z looked at Desmond's winking eye with horror.

"You have been holding out on me, Max."

"Holding out?"

"London wants names. Who is Herr Oberst?"

"Herr Oberst?"

"The man you talk to in your sleep. You have nothing to fear from this man, you know."

Z took another sip of whisky.

"Come on, Max. We know he was stationed in Stettin. We have a list of names and a picture of yourself on a stage with your SS colleagues in February '41."

Z looked at Desmond and wondered how he had managed to survive.

"Des can't help you, Max. Only you can help yourself," Cummings said with infinite patience. "Do I return to London and tell them that you won't collaborate? Is that what you want? Who is this man that you are so afraid of, Max?"

Z hesitated, then sighed heavily.

"Richter," he whispered. "His name is Bernhard Richter, SS-Obersturmbannführer Richter. He found when I was working in a field on the farm."

Thirty-six

Germany, September 1940

It was a hot sunny day as Z on his knees harvested potatoes on a farm near the Oder River. An open grey military staff car pulled up near the field and *SS-Obersturmbannführer* Richter, in his black military uniform, stepped off the road to have a pee. Pulling up his fly, he lit a cigarette standing near a solitary tree and looked across the field.

Z was hidden by a row of wooden baskets as he pulled up potatoes and tossed them into a canvas bag. He lifted his head to observe the SS man casually smoking a cigarette and suddenly stopped moving as if paralysed. The man was waving for him to come over. Z dropped down behind the row of baskets and looked behind him to see who the man might be calling. He popped his head up again and realized that the SS man in his dashing uniform was waving at him to come closer.

"*Kommen Sie näher.*"

Perhaps the man only wanted to buy a load of potatoes. Z stood up slowly, brushing dust off his overalls and emptied his potatoes into a basket, before approaching hesitantly. Richter turned to his driver and adjutant. The men were transfixed by Z's appearance.

PLAYING RUDOLF HESS

On their way back to town in the military staff car, *Obersturmbannführer* Richter and his colleagues joked with Z as they passed a bottle of schnapps among them. Sitting in the back, Richter playfully grabbed Z's canvas bag and flipped it upside down on his head. The men laughed as Z struggled to remove the bag.

"*Wie heißen Sie?*"

"Max," he replied, his voice muffled by the bag.

Richter tugged on the bag to keep it snug on Max's head.

"Keep the bag on your head, Max. That is an order."

"But it is dirty, sir," Max protested.

As Max struggled to remove the bag, Richter slapped him in the head.

"I said keep the bag on your head."

The German officers in the front seat laughed at the comic scene as they passed the bottle of schnapps.

In a SS holding cell, Max had fallen asleep on the cement floor with his head partially covered by the bag. Footsteps approached in the hallway and the cell door was opened. *Obersturmbannführer Richter* entered the cell in the company of his commanding officer. He kicked Max awake, and pulled the bag off his face.

"*Man muss es gesehen haben, um es zu glauben, Herr Oberführer* You have to see it to believe it, sir."

The bearded Oberführer looked down at the small man as Richter lit his dusty face with a torch.

"*Oh, Gott. Das ist Rudolf Hess.*"

Richter smiled at his senior officer obviously happy with his discovery of a Hess lookalike and confident for a promotion.

NICHOLAS KINSEY

Abergavenny 1942

"That was the worst day of my life," Z said, sitting with Cummings in the ward watching Desmond sleep. "I had to keep the bag on my head or they would hit me. After a time, Herr Oberst had me moved to a farmhouse where my English lessons began. A woman from Hamburg came and taught me to speak, to make conversation in English. She was a nice lady."

"What was her name?"

"Richter called her Sabrina. I don't think she was German, maybe Dutch. She laughed a lot."

Germany 1940

In a rustic farmhouse near Stettin, Z sat at a table in the kitchen near a woodstove with an English language primer and a cup of tea. Sabrina wrote on a chalkboard fixed to the wall.

"The word is 'gullible', Max. Do you have any idea what it means?"

"*Nein, Fräulein.*"

"Gullible means *leichtgläubig*. English people are gullible. They will want to believe in you. You have the face of a famous man. Another word in English is trusting, unsuspecting. It means *nichtsahnend.*"

Sabrina wrote the new words: gullible, trusting, unsuspecting on the chalkboard.

"Unsuspecting?"

Sabrina laughed loudly as footsteps were heard outside the house.

"English people are trusting, unsuspecting. They will accept you for what you are. Do not look so sad, Max. *Sie machen Fortschritte.* You are making progress."

An older man in a suit with a small SS badge on his lapel entered the room as Sabrina started to collect her things.

"Herr Bauer. Guten Tag."

"Macht Max Fortschritte?" asked Bauer.

"Ja, ja. Auf wiedersehen, Max. Herr Bauer."

The lesson was over and Sabrina hurried out, obviously not wanting to remain in the room for a moment longer than necessary with Bauer who she didn't like. As she started off on her bicycle down the muddy lane, Bauer watched her slim figure cycling away. With a lewd look on his face, he turned back to Max.

"Sabrina sieht gut aus. Nicht wahr, Max? Sabrina has a nice arse, doesn't she, Max?"

Bauer laughed and Max nodded his agreement at Bauer. The SS man sat down at the table and pulled files from a beat-up leather briefcase.

Thirty-seven

Abergavenny 1942

"In the afternoons, a man from Berlin came to tell me about Rudolf Hess: his career, his family, his political life with the Führer, his time in Egypt, everything."

Z seemed relieved to finally air his secrets to Cummings as Des snored softly nearby in the hospital ward.

"A name?" Cummings asked.

"Herr Bauer. I don't know whether it was his real name. He was very secretive. He made me repeat everything, write it down on the blackboard, then he would test me on Hess."

"How long did this go on?"

"Every day for months. We would read Hess' speeches, talk about his relationships with his wife, his friends, his family, everything."

"What about handwriting?"

"*Die Handschrift*, that was child's play, Captain. Hess wrote a lot of letters during his time in the government. First, I learned how to form each letter like Hess, then it was easy to write like him. I copied his letters hundreds of times and Herr Bauer had a handwriting expert compare my work to the work of Hess until he was satisfied."

"Where did you learn to fly?"

"Die AGO Flugzeugwerke in Oschersleben."

The AGO Aircraft factory near Magdeburg?"

"Yes, that's it."

"Who was the flight instructor?"

"A young man, Felix Hartmann, from the *Luftkriegsschule* at Berlin Gatow. A very nice man. He taught me everything I know about flying."

"So when you flew to Scotland, you flew from Magdeburg?"

"You remember the box on my map, Captain? They sent me to Aalborg in Northern Denmark where they had a Bf110. I flew southwest towards Holland, then turned northwest and joined the Hess flight plan."

"So that was it. You never needed to refuel?"

"I had lots of fuel, Captain."

"One final point, Max. Who was the Oberführer in the prison cell with Richter?"

"I only saw his face for a moment."

"What was his name, Max?"

"I don't know. I remember Richter once called him Wolfram. They seemed to be close friends. He had a beard."

"Very good, Max. Thank you. I think it's time we left."

Z and Cummings stood up quietly as Desmond napped fixing them with his wandering eye. Cummings squeezed Desmond's hand, but the young man didn't wake up.

"Bye, Des."

In the local pub, Lt May stood at the bar ordering a pint from Toby, the barman. After he paid for his lager, he left his copy of the *Western Mail* with the headlines 'Rommel Counter-attacks at El Alamein' on the bar near Guy Ramsey, a London journalist in a pinstripe suit and trench coat, and went over to sit at a corner table. Ramsey finished his drink, put on his fedora, and stopped near May's table.

"I believe this is yours. Good day, sir."

May picked up the newspaper and pocketed a brown envelope from within. He sipped his lager as he read the paper.

Standing behind the bar, Toby turned up the sound on the BBC news report: "Now to North Africa, Allied forces have broken through German and Italian lines at El Alamein and General Montgomery has won a stunning victory over Axis forces in the Western Desert. The Allies have pushed General Rommel's forces back to El Agheila with huge German and Italian losses. It is estimated that Axis forces lost 75,000 men, 500 tanks and 1000 guns in the battle. General Rommel is destroying equipment and laying mines in a desperate retreat toward Tunisia as the Eighth Army pursues their advance to the West."

The men at the bar sounded a loud hurrah and clapped their hands as the news report continued.

"Prime Minister Winston Churchill has ordered church bells to ring across the nation and announced: "This is not the end, it is not even the beginning of the end. But it is, perhaps, the end of the beginning."

"Free drinks on me," yelled a man at the bar.

"Have you heard the news, Toby?" a woman asked, stepping out of the back office. "Bloody Rommel has been beaten in North Africa."

"Of course, I have Mary," Toby replied, grinning. "Old Liam's buying a round of drinks for everyone to celebrate. The last time he bought a round of drinks was during the Great War."

"The Afrika Korps is finished," Lt Malone said as Mozart played on the gramophone on the verandah. "That's what the papers are saying, sir."

"No, that is not possible, Lieutenant," Z said, touching up a sketch of the two greyhound dogs pulling on their leashes on Sugar Loaf Mountain. "Rommel will be back. He is unbeatable. It is because of the Italians that he lost at El Alamein. They are not good soldiers."

"You may be right, sir, but I think Rommel is a bit over-extended in North Africa," Malone said. "They say the supply lines are way too long for the Wehrmacht to have any traction. Did you know that the Captain's brother Brian is serving with the 8th Army under Montgomery?"

"No, he never mentioned it," Z replied.

A knock came at the door as Dr Dicks arrived for a visit accompanied by Captain Cummings and an older gentleman.

"You seem to be well installed in your new digs, Herr Hess?" Dicks said.

"Yes, sir. It is good here, but very noisy."

"This is my colleague, Major Ellis Jones. He will be looking after you while I am away."

The major, an elderly military doctor from the Pen-y-Fal mental hospital, stepped forward to shake Z's hand.

"Good day, Herr Hess."

"*Guten Morgen*," Z replied.

"What noises are you talking about?" Dicks asked, looking at Z's White Castle sketch propped up against the wall and absentmindedly picking up a Dinky Toys model airplane from the table.

"Don't touch that, sir," Z warned.

"This is a Me109 fighter. Is it the same plane you arrived in,

Herr Hess?"

"Mine was a Me110, Dr Dicks. The Me110 is a twin-engine heavy fighter with a longer wingspan than the ME109."

Dicks put down the toy plane.

"So, what sort of noises are you hearing?"

"The trains make a terrible noise day and night. It is impossible to sleep," Z said.

Cummings sat down near Z and added: "There is a marshalling yard next door. Trains coming south from Manchester pass through Hereford and Abergavenny, then go on to the South coast, sir."

"Have you heard the whistles? No one can get used to the whistles," Z complained. "It is not only the trains. They are banging pots and pans in the kitchen in the early morning, anything to make noise."

Cummings shared a nod with Dicks, who was looking at the title of a book on the table.

"You are reading Goethe's *Dichtung und Wahrheit*?"

"I am studying it," Z murmured, annoyed by Dicks' intrusion into his private life.

"I have word concerning your colleagues in Germany," Dicks said. "You remember Alfred and Karlheinz. Alfred Leitgen and Karlheinz Pintsch, your adjutants. They were both arrested after your arrival in this country."

"Alfred? Karlheinz?"

"Not just your adjutants, your secretaries Hildegard Fath and Ingeborg Sperr. They have all been jailed."

"Who are these people? I don't remember them."

"Come on, Herr Hess. They were your friends. You were close to them. Remember Josef Platzer, your manservant. Rudi Lippert. He worked for you. He is in jail, too."

"I don't remember any of these names."

Dicks looked sceptical.

"Herr Hess, do you think you might remember their faces?" Ellis Jones asked.

"Their faces?"

"Yes, sometimes we might not remember the name, but we will recognize a face."

"No, I don't think so."

Ellis Jones raised an eyebrow and looked at Dicks just as Malone ran into the room holding a copy of the London *Daily Mail*. He pulled Cummings aside.

"Sir, have you seen this? There is an article on Hess on the front page."

Cummings held up the paper showing the headlines:

THE STORY ALL BRITAIN HAS AWAITED
by Guy Ramsey

A look of shock crossed Cummings' face. He turned the paper to show it to Dicks and Ellis Jones.

Thirty-eight

Berlin 1973

"The front page article in the London *Daily Mail* went into great detail about Z's daily routine and psychological condition. It created an uproar in Parliament and enraged the Foreign Office who were trying to keep Z under wraps. The PM's war cabinet fumed at the article."

At the *biergarten* in Berlin, Terry listened with rapt attention as Cummings continued.

"A mob of newspaper reporters descended on Abergavenny and had to be trucked out of town by the dozen. Not long after the public outrage at Hess' easy life in detention died down, Parliament raised the question of war crimes and whether the prisoner would be tried in a public forum and sentenced."

"As you can imagine, it didn't take us long to find the reporter's inside source," Cummings said.

Abergavenny 1942

Captain Cummings sat at his desk in the Maindiff hospital office when two soldiers brought in Lt May who slumped down in a chair.

"Thank you, gentlemen. Please wait outside."

The men left the room as Cummings observed May who was unshaven and had slept in his clothes.

"Why'd you do it, Lieutenant?"

"Don't know, sir."

"What did the journalist promise you?"

"Just the money, sir."

"What did Ramsey want to know?"

"We only talked once to set it up when I was still at Mytchett, then I left him notes about the daily routine here."

"The daily routine?"

"Yeah, he wanted to know what was going on with Hess. Like what the miserable bastard was getting up to."

"So he wasn't pressing you for any particular information?"

"No, sir, just general things like the food, the walks, what he was reading, listening to on the radio, stuff like that."

"You're going to pay a high price for your indiscretions, Lieutenant. You'll be cleaning latrines in a POW camp somewhere in Scotland for the foreseeable future. You also risk jail time."

"Yes, sir."

The captain stood up and led May out of the office, where the soldiers took charge of him.

Claudia was at the back of the house, putting out the laundry on the washing line, when she heard a woman's voice nearby.

"I seen your husband with that Hess fellah, ma'am."

Claudia turned to see an older woman sticking her head through the hedgerow. Her face and hair had a yellow-orange glow.

"Hello, you must be our neighbour?"

"Twenty-odd years, ma'am. My Willy works down at the yard on them locomotives."

"I'm Claudia, Paul Cummings' wife. You are?"

"Williams, ma'am. I'm Catrin. I saw your husband's name in the paper."

Claudia put out the last of the washing as she listened to Catrin.

"The Welshman ain't got nothin' against the Nazis," Catrin said. "My son is working over at the Mardy camp and he says they're right honourable young fellahs. He's talkin' to them Nazis every day."

"Not every German soldier is a Nazi, Mrs Williams. A lot of them are very nice young men."

"You're German, but you're a WAAC. I seen your uniform."

"Yes, I am."

"We are not like the bloody Irish, neutral and all. There's no work in Ireland, so many of 'em are comin' over here to work in our factories. Everybody in this town has a job 'cause of the war."

"Do you work in a factory, Mrs Williams?"

"Yeah, you seen me 'Canary' yellow?"

"Yes, I heard about the sulphur."

"Lots of us have it. They call us 'Canaries' or 'Canary girls' down at the shop. We're fillin' shells and mines all day long with TNT. See, it's yellow coloured and you gotta fill each shell with the stuff. Then you put in the tube for the detonator and it gets on your face and hair. What's the name of your kid?"

"Steffi, she's four years old."

"Isn't she a cute one? Well, I must go. You need anythin' at all, ma'am. You just knock on my door and I'll help you the best I can."

"Thank you, Mrs Williams. That's very kind of you," Claudia said as the neighbour's face disappeared from the hedgerow.

After a late meal, Claudia joined Cummings in the living room after having put Steffi to bed. Cummings was drinking ersatz coffee and listening quietly to the radio.

"You think it will blow over?" Claudia asked.

"I don't know. Major Foley is coming down tomorrow. They may want to curtail our walks with Max for a while."

"The article describes the man's daily routine at Maindiff. I don't see why it should impact our operation."

"People think of him as a war criminal and want him in a POW camp," Cummings said. "They are shocked by the relaxed conditions of confinement."

"But Paul, you've delivered on Hess. The operation is a success."

"I agree. We have been very successful, and the major knows it. I think the problem is that the Foreign Office may not like the message and want to shoot the messenger."

In the early morning, Lt Malone was asleep in his bed when he heard a cry from Z's room. He stumbled out of bed, stopped to listen a moment and heard a second muffled cry. He ran down the hall and entered the bedroom where he found Z curled up on the floor.

"What's wrong?"

"*Magenschmerzen*. Stomach upset," Z winced, clearly in pain. Malone kneeled close to Z.

"A hot water bottle might ease the pain, sir."

"*Ja, gut.* Please."

Malone ran off to fetch the hot-water bottle, leaving Z grimacing on the floor.

A group of waiting journalists rushed to the curb as a staff car arrived at the main entrance to the Maindiff Court Hospital. Major Foley and Captain Cummings got out of the car, followed by Colonel John Rawlings Rees, consulting psychiatrist to the British Army. Foley and Cummings were both in uniform, while Rees was elegantly dressed in a pinstripe suit. The men ignored the shouted questions from the reporters and hurried up the steps.

"Colonel Rees, would you like to make a statement, sir?" asked a journalist who had recognized the famous psychiatrist.

"A statement, please, sir."

"Any news about Hess?"

The men entered the Maindiff lobby and were met by Dr Dicks and Major Ellis Jones, who led the Colonel into the prisoner's wing. As they entered the verandah, Rees stepped forward to shake hands with Z in his dressing gown slouched on the couch.

"I'm sorry, sir," Z said. "I have decided not to shake hands with anyone until the war is over."

Although Rees didn't appear to be offended by the prisoner's behaviour, Dicks looked thoroughly annoyed.

"How are you feeling these days, Herr Hess?" Rees asked.

"Not good, sir. I have stomach pains."

"When do you get these pains?"

"I had one this morning early. The lieutenant brought me a hot water bottle."

"Malone said he was lying on the floor for some twenty minutes," Dr Dicks said.

"Are they all like this?" Rees inquired.

"Some last a long time."

"The major told me he gave you belladonna to help with the pain, but you refused to take the pills?" Rees inquired.

Z remained silent and then replied: "I have always been against any kind of medicine."

Ellis Jones stepped forward and said: "I offered him soap and water enemas to help ease the attacks, but he refused them, sir?"

"An enema's no good," the prisoner said. "I want to leave the poison in my bowels so that the International Commission will find it at my autopsy."

Dicks raised his eyebrows in silent fury.

"It has been reported to me you are losing your memory," Rees asked. "Is that true, sir?"

"I cannot recall certain things. Sometimes they just seem to float off into a grey fog. There are many things I can't remember."

"We have methods to treat amnesia. These methods can bring back your memories. Dr Dicks here is an expert in treating memory loss. I'm sure he can help you."

Z looked around warily at Dr Dicks.

"Colonel, have you met General Von Thoma, who was captured at El Alamein?" Z asked.

"No, I have not."

"I read that General Von Thoma dined with General Montgomery. They talked about the battle."

"I did not know that. Why do you ask?"

Z remained silent.

"Are you lacking companionship here at Maindiff?" Rees

asked with genuine concern. "Do you feel lonely?"

"No, sir. I have Lt Malone and Captain Cummings to look after me. It is better that I remain here by myself."

Thirty-nine

Major Foley and Captain Cummings walked around the Maindiff hospital perimeter, examining potential breaches of security. They arrived at Z's enclosed garden at the back of the hospital.

"This is where that man Marek climbed up," Cummings said. "We will put up a tarp to prevent people from seeing into the garden."

"Good."

"I think the increased security will keep the reporters and photographers away, sir, but I am not so sure that an ill-intentioned German agent can be stopped."

"This is a hospital, after all, Captain. Not a secure POW camp. We can only do so much under the circumstances."

They walked on, disappearing through the trees.

"We could use narco-analysis, but I seriously doubt he will accept it coming from me," Dr Dicks said to Colonel Rees and Major Ellis Jones standing in the doorway to the hospital clinic.

"There are risks involved using Evipan," Ellis Jones said.

"Major, I have used it dozens of times with no problems and it has been very useful," Dicks replied.

"What is your diagnosis, Colonel?" Ellis Jones asked Rees.

"I think it is most probably hysterical amnesia, very similar to what our soldiers develop when they come home. A self-protective mechanism," Rees replied. "It must cause him some anguish when he can't remember things. Major, perhaps you can convince him to take the treatment."

"Of course, sir," Ellis Jones said. "I will ask him and see what he says."

"Well, thank you, gentlemen. Let's keep in touch," Colonel Rees said as he left to catch a train.

"We will do our best, sir," Dicks replied.

"Has Major Foley left, sir?"

Captain Cummings looked up from his desk in the Maindiff office.

"Yes, Lieutenant. A car came to collect him."

Malone appeared to be uneasy about something.

"Sir, I have been working with you for over a year," Malone said. "It is not my business to ask questions, but I think you are not really a captain with the Scots Guards, are you?"

"You would be right, Malone. I was given the promotion last year to facilitate my work at Mytchett House with the prisoner."

"Mr Hess said you are a spook. Are you a spook, sir?"

"You might say so, Lieutenant."

"And Major Foley, sir?"

"Yes, Malone, but keep it under your hat."

"Don't worry about me, sir. I know how to keep a secret."

Malone went to the hot plate in the corner and poured himself a cup of tea.

"Like some tea, sir?"

"Yes, thank you."

"For a spook, you are a nice bloke, sir."

Cummings looked up from a report.

"Thank you, Malone. So are you."

"I don't know why you care so much about the man," Claudia asked.

Cummings was shaving in the bathroom while Claudia packed their bags in the bedroom. The radio played *Falling in Love Again* by Marlene Dietrich.

"It is strange, but Max makes me think of my cousin Freddie. You know he was a bit naive, always on about something. A foot soldier for any cause. You never met him. He was killed in Spain in '37 with the International brigade."

"We are not supposed to take a personal interest, Paul. You tell me that all the time. Max is just another German agent here under false pretenses."

"You are right, darling, but Max is a special case. I am sure he was in awe of Herr Oberst and ready to do anything for the cause. He is so trusting and loyal."

"Well, I remember one of those fellows at the safe house on Crespigny Road, a Nazi fanatic."

"Yes, I am sure you do. You got into a shouting match with the bastard and I had to get you away before you attacked him. Those are usually the ones that end up hanging from a rope in Pentonville Prison."

"Spies are spies, Paul. There is always something a little fanatical about these people. Not everyone can be turned. There are people whose loyalty is forever."

"But Max is different. He did not volunteer, you know."

"He is just as fanatical, Paul. When are you expecting

Malone with the car?"

"He should be here soon."

Claudia folded the last of her clothes from the closet as the song with Marlene Dietrich's smoky, hypnotic voice wound down on the radio.

"Falling in love again
Never wanted to
What am I to do?
Can't help it.

Love's always been my game
Play it how I may
I was made that way
Can't help it.

Men cluster to me
like moths around a flame
And if their wings burn
I know I'm not to blame."

"That song always brings tears to my eyes. I miss my old life before the war."

Cummings stepped out of the bathroom, drying his face with a towel and kissed Claudia.

"We didn't have a care in those days, did we, darling?"

"We didn't have Steffi. We are lucky to have Steffi, but this war is so tiresome," Claudia said as tears welled up in her eyes.

A BBC news report came up on the radio. The announcer read:

"News from the Russian front. Field Marshal Paulus of the

Sixth Army has surrendered at Stalingrad to Soviet forces after being surrounded for over two months. Herr Hitler, who had sworn that the German Army would never leave Stalingrad, had ordered the Sixth Army to remain in the city while an air bridge was organized to supply them. Field Marshal Paulus surrendered with 22 generals and 90,000 men. This is a significant victory for our Russian allies."

"I knew it. That stupid man has done it," Claudia said. "He will lose his army and bring all hell down on Germany. The country will be destroyed."

"I agree, darling, the war is lost for Germany. It is very sad for the German people, but they brought it on themselves. The tide is turning with the Russians winning battles. This is very good news for the Allies. We better get a move on."

It was a cold winter day as a military staff car pulled up to the house and Lt Malone stepped out from the driver's seat. He was met by Cummings, wearing civilian clothes and carrying two suitcases.

"Morning, sir."

"Hello, Lieutenant," Cummings said, putting the bags down near the car. "Claudia and I are going to miss Wales. It's back to dirty old London."

"We'll miss you, sir."

"I'll miss the Scots Guards, Malone."

Claudia appeared at the front door with a carry-on and Steffi clutching a teddy bear.

"We'll miss you too, Lieutenant," Claudia said. "It was always a pleasure working with you."

"Thank you, Mrs Cummings," Malone said. "I have a small present for Steffi."

Malone picked up a cardboard box from the front seat and put it in the hands of the child. Steffi smiled with anticipation as she pulled off the top of the box.

"Mama, it's an airplane," she squealed.

"It's a Dinky Toy," Malone said, "a present from Mr Hess and me."

"That's wonderful, Steffi. Isn't that nice?" Claudia said.

Claudia raised her eyebrows, not at all convinced of the suitability of the toy.

"It's a Me109 like the plane that brought Mr Hess to Scotland." Cummings said to Steffi.

"Actually, I bought it for Mr Hess a while back, but he doesn't want it anymore. He says a Me109 is not a Me110, so we thought Steffi might like it."

"I like it," Steffi said as she launched the plane into a steep dive.

"Thank you so much, Lieutenant," Claudia said. "Steffi is a funny girl, she likes planes, trains and lorries."

"I think she is going to be a fighter pilot one day," Cummings mused with pride. "We better be off. I have to make a stop at Maindiff before we leave town."

Malone slammed the boot closed as the family got in the car.

At Maindiff hospital, Cummings found Z eating his breakfast on the verandah and listening to Mozart on the gramophone in the company of Lt Fenton.

"I am off to London with the family, Herr Hess."

Z stood up to say goodbye.

"I will miss you, Captain."

"I am sure Fenton and Malone will take good care of you, sir."

"Righto, Captain," Fenton said.

"Thank you. Thank you for everything," Z said.

"You know you can always write to me."

Z nodded as Cummings shook hands with Fenton and embraced Z before leaving.

Forty

"You know your amnesia is not incurable, sir," Major Ellis Jones said to Z as they walked around the hospital grounds accompanied by Dr Dicks.

"Are you sure?" Z asked.

"The best treatment is the injection. This will allow you to get back those memories from your youth, growing up in Egypt, your summers in Bavaria with your family," Ellis Jones pursued nonchalantly.

"And what extraordinary memories you have, Herr Hess. Your life with the Führer," Dr Dicks added.

"The Führer?"

"You were with him at Landsberg prison, at the party rally in Nuremberg in 1934. You were his Deputy *Reichsminister*. What an extraordinary accomplishment!"

"I don't remember any of it."

"Do you remember jumping with a parachute from an airplane?"

"No?"

"Imagine if you could remember the jump and flying the plane solo," Dicks said.

Z paused for a moment, a confused look on his face.

"I feel like I am living in a fog. I can hardly remember what

213

happened yesterday."

London 1943

It was a cold day in February as a London taxi deposited the Cummings family at the door of a rundown, two-up two-down row house in Islington. Claudia and Cummings looked at each other, the disappointment palpable on their faces.

Cummings tried the key in the lock and, after playing with it, managed to open the door. Claudia and Steffi entered a narrow hallway as Cummings followed with several bags and three large suitcases. They looked at the green paint on the walls and the threadbare carpet on the stairs leading to the rooms above and remembered their lovely house in Abergavenny. Steffi led the way down the narrow hall to the kitchen at the back of the house, where they discovered broken dishes and animal droppings on the floor.

"*Scheiße*," Claudia howled. "This place is a bloody awful dump, Paul. Look, a cat has been shitting on the floor."

"Mama, don't say that," Steffi corrected her mother. "You always tell me to speak proper English."

"You are right, *Schatzi*. We mustn't talk that way."

Paul smiled at his daughter.

"Let me take a look around, darling," Cummings said. "We need to get the heat going. I'll start the furnace."

Cummings went to look for the wayward cat and found a broken window in the living room off the kitchen. He stuffed a cushion in the hole to stop the blast of cold air.

He descended the wooden stairs to the furnace room in the basement. In the dim light, he pulled open the furnace door and stuffed old newspaper and pieces of wood in the stove. He lit the paper and tossed a few lumps of coal on the wood. As he stood up, he noticed a rat running past the stove.

"Bloody hell, we've got rats too, damn it," Cummings murmured to himself, wondering how he was going to break the news to Claudia. Perhaps it would be best to wait a day or two until they had settled in.

Abergavenny 1943

In the prisoner's quarters, Z was drawing an exotic bird from a photograph when Major Ellis Jones entered the room.

"Good morning, Herr Hess. How are you?"

"I'm fine, Major."

"What about the injection, sir? Colonel Rees and Dr Dicks think it will improve your memory."

"You think so?" Z asked, turning his attention to his drawing.

"The technique has been very effective on other patients and Dr Dicks swears by it, sir."

"I think I will wait until I return to Germany. I prefer a natural cure, Major."

"Dr Dicks is leaving for London tonight, so this is your last chance."

"I would like to be repatriated, Major," Z said. "With my medical condition, do you think the government might send me home on that Swedish hospital ship? I read in the newspaper that the S/S Drottningholm was in Liverpool recently."

"Yes, but I think the ship is only for wounded German POWs, the seriously ill, the incurable. I hardly think..."

Z interrupted the major.

"But Colonel Rees could authorize it, couldn't he, sir? You could ask him for me."

"I will mention your request to the colonel, Herr Hess."

"Thank you, Major."

Ellis Jones left the prisoner to his sketching.

Forty-one

Suffolk 1943

Cummings heard the airplane first. He reached over to wake up his driver who had drifted off during the long waiting hours. A two-seat, Folke-Wulf 44 biplane flew over the coastal town in the dead of night. The two men watched the trajectory of the small plane crossing the sky.

The driver started the car, illuminating the hedgerows bordering the country lane and accelerated away only to cut the lights as they turned a corner. They were soon racing along a narrow country road in the direction of the biplane.

In a field several miles away, a German agent rolled up his parachute and buried it near a hedgerow. He stealthily moved across the field carrying his radio transmitter in a rucksack along with a Luger semi-automatic pistol, a knife, some English currency and the address of a house where he was to rendezvous with a contact.

"Where the hell is he?" Cummings asked as his driver

pulled up in the lane. They quickly turned the car around and raced off the way they had come, looking for the enemy agent.

"We should have seen his parachute, sir."

"We missed him. He's on the ground now, looking for shelter. He'll be hard to find."

At a nearby pub, several Home Guard officers were gathered waiting for stragglers from the Local Defence Volunteers to join them. The Home Guard known as "Dad's Army" was made up of men ineligible for military service for medical reasons or due to their age.

As the last of the men arrived, some of them still drunk or half asleep at this hour in the early morning, they started marching down the country lane led by Captain McCann.

"Corporal Walker, where is your weapon?" McCann asked, furious at the lack of discipline in his unit.

"I wasn't at home, sir, when I got the call."

"Off with his lady friend, no doubt," laughed Walker's friend Corporal Barker.

"Shut up, Barker," Walker replied.

The men marched around a bend in the road in the moonless, pitch-black night.

As the night fog rolled in from the North Sea, Cummings and his driver parked in a field, quietly waiting for the German agent to show himself.

"He has to come this way," Cummings announced.

"Yes, sir."

"How far are we from Wickham?"

"Just a few miles, sir. We can't miss him on this road."

The German agent headed down the same road watching for traffic, unconcerned that men were out searching for him. As he approached the town, he heard the platoon of Home Guard coming his way and jumped over a stone wall into a field. The HG men approached noisily. Walker, who had stopped to light a cigarette allowing his colleagues to get ahead of him, heard a noise nearby and stopped to listen.

In the field, the German agent was flat on his back after slipping in the mud. He looked up at several cows near a barn and a water tank. He scrambled to his feet and moved towards the barn.

In the lane, Walker hurried to catch up with Captain McCann.

"I heard a noise in the field over there, Captain," Walker whispered to McCann.

The captain silently pulled his men together and ordered them over the wall into the field. The men spread out, with half the men flanking the barn as the fog thickened.

Walker bumped into Barker from behind.

"Keep your distance, you tosser," Barker whispered.

"I can't see fuck all," Walker complained as he stumbled forward, trying to keep up.

Barker took another step forward and slipped in the mud, nearly losing his balance. His finger tightened on the trigger of his Enfield P-17 rifle and suddenly the rifle went off.

"What the fuck!" Walker said to his colleague. "You seen the bastard?"

"No, dammit. I slipped," Barker said.

The excited HG men fired blindly into the fog, barely missing each other and unaware that they had inadvertently caught the German agent in a wild crossfire.

The agent grabbed the pistol in his rucksack. He was

experienced in undercover operations but had never been under such a sustained attack. These Englishmen were crazy firing their guns in a fog. He reckoned they must be untrained recruits without a clue. He prayed silently crouching in the ditch, hoping that these men would soon give up the chase.

Cummings and his driver drove off in the direction of the gunshots searching for the German parachutist. As they approached the area, they heard a new barrage of fire coming from a field. They pulled over and got out of the car to listen.

Corporal Barker, who prided himself as being the best shot in the entire unit, was embarrassed that he had accidentally discharged his weapon. The fog was starting to clear as he advanced slowly, followed by Walker a few feet behind him. They sneaked up behind a cow near the barn.

As the fog was lifting, the German agent became more and more desperate. He stood up and tried to break out of the circle of HG men by running into the shadows. He ran right towards Barker and Walker, wildly firing his pistol. Seeing the German running towards them, Barker dropped into a kneeling position and, with no hesitation, fired one deadly shot.

"How far away were you when you dropped him?" a policeman asked.

"About 20 to 30 yards," Barker replied.

"You must be a good shot, Corporal," a second policeman added.

"He's more than a good shot. He's a bloody marksman," Walker said. "Barker shot the bastard between the eyes as he was running at us."

The dawn light was coming up as the ragtag unit of HG men passed a flask of whisky and celebrated their success with laughter and loud voices near an ambulance parked in the lane. The men were clearly elated to have brought down a German agent in a gunfight.

Inside the ambulance, a local doctor examined the body of the dead German as Cummings went through the personal effects in the rucksack, looking for clues to his identity. He collected the rucksack and transmitter and returned to his car.

"It's a pity we lost the man, sir," commented the driver as Cummings put the rucksack on the backseat and got in.

"Bloody fools firing at each other in the dark. We lost a man and probably some serious intelligence."

Forty-two

Abergavenny 1943

"Lovely day for a walk, sir. You remember you had a panic attack out here last year," Major Ellis Jones reminded Z as they walked through the heather and bracken on Sugar Loaf mountain.

"A panic attack?" Z asked, wearing his flat cap and red scarf. "But Major, I have never been out here before. I would remember the castle."

"You don't remember the panic attack, sir?"

Ellis Jones quietly walked on to avoid confronting Z too directly. He doubted seriously that the man could forget such a traumatic event. Z stopped walking and looked clearly confused as Lt Malone arrived with the two greyhounds pulling on a leash. Below them, Lt Fenton followed at a distance, carrying a Sten gun.

"The captain told me you couldn't stand up and were writhing on the ground, sir," Ellis Jones said. "You felt nauseous, dizzy. The captain had to help you walk down. You must remember that."

"I don't remember. I don't remember this place."

"Lt Malone, you have been up here many times with Herr

Hess and the dogs, haven't you?" Ellis Jones asked.

"Yes, sir. Mr Hess has sketches of the castle and the dogs in his room. Don't you, sir?"

Z remained silent.

"You really should submit to treatment, Herr Hess," Ellis Jones said. "It must be terrible for you not to be able to remember these things."

London 1943

Major Foley sat in the dark smoking a pipe near a covered bar and fieldstone fireplace in the garden. The safe house was quite unremarkable, a row house with on one side a bombed-out warehouse and on the other an abandoned building. Light from an interior room spilled into the yard through blackout drapes. Inside, three men were sitting at a table interrogating a suspect. A bright light was directed on the man's sweaty face and from time to time, voices were raised in anger.

Captain Cummings entered the yard, and the major stood up to greet him.

"It's nice to have you back, Paul. Would you like a drink, a whisky or perhaps a sherry?"

"Sherry. It's good to see you again, sir."

The major got up to pour the drinks from a small wet bar. He returned with the drinks and handed Cummings his sherry after having refreshed his whisky. He proceeded to light his pipe with an ember from the fire in the hearth.

"Cloak and dagger work isn't all it is cut out to be," Foley said. "Long hours waiting in the cold and dark for some bloody nonsense to happen, dealing with infuriating people and often failure at the end of the road. That's our lot doing our bit for His Majesty's service. I heard about the cock-up, Paul."

"The bloody Home Guard, sir. They are the weakest link."

"The headlines were almost worth it: the HG defending the country from Nazi agents. I heard the PM loved it. Corporal Barker is a war hero with his picture in the paper."

"It was complete chaos, sir," Cummings said. "Men shooting in every direction in a dense fog. Luckily, no member of the Guard was killed. Any news about our Polish butcher, sir?"

"We couldn't get anything from the man. The Russians made no attempt to claim him. He was hanged last week at Pentonville prison. I only hope there aren't any more attempts on our man's life."

"Yes, sir."

"Speaking of the Russians. You read the papers so you know about the Pravda article that caused such a stir last year."

"Yes, I heard about that."

"The Russians summoned our ambassador in Moscow for a talk after Pravda reported that Britain was a haven for Nazi gangsters. They accused us of providing diplomatic immunity to Hess as Hitler's representative in Britain. They demanded that we try the man and hang him as soon as possible."

"Yes, I remember hearing the story."

"At the time there was a good deal of pressure on Parliament to comply with the Russian demand. The government was worried that the Russians might sue for a separate peace with Germany, but now that we seem to be winning the war, the pressure is off."

"I don't see why the Russians feel so threatened by the presence of Hess in Britain. Stalin was still at peace with

Germany when Hess flew to Scotland."

"Yes, that's true, Paul, but Stalin fears the same thing we do. That Britain and its allies might make a separate peace with Hitler."

Foley finished his drink.

"And that's why I think this Marek chap was NKVD. Kill Hess and the problem goes away."

"Yes, I can see that. It makes sense, but we will never have any proof now that Marek is dead."

"Welcome to the world of intelligence gathering, Paul.

Foley lit his pipe again.

"You have done some excellent work for us, Paul. Remember Wolfram, the Oberführer? We have identified him. He is Himmler's man, Wolfram Sievers. General Secretary of the *Ahnenerbe*, the scientific chaps behind the Aryan race studies. *Ahnenerbe* means 'inheritance of the forefathers'. You know they conducted several anthropological studies on Nordic peoples. All scientific claptrap, if you don't mind me saying so."

"So you think Himmler was involved?"

"With Sievers behind the subterfuge, you can be sure Himmler financed the project. Months of intensive training, unlimited funds. Sievers couldn't have done it alone. We think that Himmler has been scheming for some time to replace Hitler and to sue for peace."

"So Himmler had his colleague Hess executed somewhere in Northern Germany?" Cummings asked.

"That would seem to be the case. It is quite brilliant, really. Have Hess land at a secluded airbase, kill him and then replace the *Reichsminister* with a decoy flying from Denmark. I think you may be up for a promotion shortly. I doubt we could have gotten it all with our methods."

It was late at night as Cummings returned to the row house. He crept inside silently in case Claudia had gone to bed. From the hallway, he could see a light on in the kitchen and a man lying under the sink with a pipe wrench and a torch. He went to the kitchen and found Claudia sitting on a chair in her dressing gown.

"What happened, Claudia?" Cummings asked, entering a disaster zone with water on the floor and a bucket in the corner with wet towels everywhere.

The plumber slid out from under the sink.

"The lady had a little accident, gov'ner, a pipe burst."

Claudia was fuming as she got up to pour the tea.

"The water pressure has been off and on, sir," the plumber said. "With the bombing, the pipes suffer something awful."

"Here's your tea, Mr Clark," Claudia said, putting the cup and saucer on the counter.

"Thank you, ma'am."

Claudia left the room, ignoring her husband.

"Won't be long, sir. Be done in a jiffy," Clark said.

"Thank you for coming by so late, Mr Clark."

"The demand has been non-stop, sir. We get breaks in the line and burst pipes at all hours of the night."

"I'm sure you do."

Cummings left the plumber to his work and exited the room. He found Claudia in a huff sitting on the stairs leading to the second-floor bedrooms.

"I'm sorry, Paul. This has just been too much. The move to this dump, the rats and now burst pipes."

"How did it happen?"

"I was asleep in the bedroom when I heard a bang downstairs. I came into the kitchen and the water was everywhere. I managed to stuff a rag in the pipe to slow the water and I called the plumber."

"I'm sorry, darling. I know this house is a disappointment."

"Why can't you ask the major to put in a word for us?"

"I will, I will. The major is looking into a promotion for me for our work in Wales."

"That's wonderful, *Liebling*, but it doesn't get us a new place. Get Foley to call MI5 and request a meeting with 'Housekeeping'. We deserve better than this."

"I think it was either this place in Islington or somewhere outside central London, with an hour of travel time."

"I am sure they can do better. Just ask them. You never complain, Paul, so they don't care what they give you."

"Yes, I will. I hear the office wants you back at work with Werner and Martin next week."

"Another week like this in this bloody house with the exterminators and the plumber, I think I will go mad."

Abergavenny 1943

Major Ellis Jones popped into Z's room while the prisoner was reading a book.

"So, how are you feeling today?"

"Better, the walking is good for me."

"Dr Dicks is worried about your memory loss. He thinks you should have the injection, Herr Hess. He is coming down to talk to you."

"I think I will practice mental training to get back my memory. That is the natural way, is it not, Major?"

"I am not sure that would be effective in your case, sir."

"I have been forgetting things for some time now. It doesn't really matter whether I can remember what I have done before. So long as I can read, draw and amuse myself to pass the time, I am happy."

He smiled at Ellis Jones, having fun with the older man.

"When I return to Germany, the memory loss will pass or perhaps I will find some treatment. If I were to remember everything that has happened to me, it might not be very pleasant. So I prefer to wait and see how things go."

"It is your decision, Herr Hess. I am only here to provide support. Good day, sir."

Ellis Jones left Z to his reading.

Forty-three

Berlin 1973

"Z's amnesia was driving the doctors crazy," Cummings said, looking out at the Tiergarten Lake. In the afternoon heat, Cummings and Terry were in shirtsleeves watching the ducks on the water.

"Colonel Rees declared in his reports that Z showed signs of mental illness that could only compromise a war crimes tribunal," Cummings said. "The Foreign Office was furious. Dicks and Ellis Jones pestered Z for several months to take the treatment and finally succeeded in convincing him to voluntarily accept narco-analysis. He was given Evipan, a hexobarbital drug similar to the truth drug Sodium Amytal."

Abergavenny 1944

"*Hundert, neunundneunzig, achtundneunzig, siebenundneunzig, sechsundneunzig, fünfundneunzig...*"

Z counted backwards from 100 lying on the operating table in the Maindiff clinic as Major Ellis Jones injected 5 1/2 cc of the anaesthetic into his arm.

Dr Dicks, who knew his presence often annoyed the patient, entered the room and watched as Ellis Jones finished injecting the Evipan. In case of an overreaction to the drug, Dicks had a syringe of Coramine ready on the trolley.

"Dreiundachtzig, zweiundachtzig, einundachtzig..."

Z's voice slackened, and he ceased to count. His muscles appeared relaxed and he started to snore. Dicks checked Z's pulse and took note of the heart rate. The man shivered and his facial muscles twitched, but he appeared to be in a deep sleep. Ellis Jones fetched a blanket to cover his legs and chest.

Dicks led the questioning in a gentle voice.

"You will now be able to recall all the names and faces of your dear ones. Your memory will return. We are here to help you."

Z's face twitched as he listened to the doctor's voice.

"Where are you?"

"I'm home. It is a birthday party. Dieter is 30 years old."

There was a pause as Dicks wrote down Z's reply on a notepad.

"How old are you?"

"I am forty-five. There are 15 years between Dieter and me."

"Is your brother Alfred there?"

"No."

"Your sister Margarete?"

"No."

"Your mother?"

"Yes, my mother, my brother and his best friend, Franz Bieber."

"What else can you remember?"

"We are singing songs. Dieter and Franz look very smart in their uniforms. My mother and I admire them."

NICHOLAS KINSEY

Germany 1939

The living room and kitchen area of the modest Hörner home were festooned with Nazi regalia as Dieter and Franz sang their party songs, getting drunk on glasses of schnapps.

"Vorwärts! Vorwärts! Schmettern die hellen Fanfaren
Vorwärts! Vorwärts! Jugend kennt keine Gefahren.
Deutschland, du wirst leuchtend stehn,
Mögen wir auch untergehn.

(Forward! Forward! Blare the bright fanfares
Forward! Forward! Youth has no fear,
Germany, you shall stand radiant,
Even if we shall fail.)

Max watched Dieter and Franz celebrating as he drank tea with his mother, Frieda, who was busy darning a sock. She found the two young men immensely charming in their new SS uniforms while Max felt ill at ease imagining his half-brother going off to war.

Abergavenny 1944

In the Maindiff clinic, the questions continued.
"Where is your father?"
"He is dead."
"When did he die?"
"During the Great War."
Dicks looked at Ellis Jones and frowned. He knew that Johann Fritz Hess had died in '41. It had been reported in the

German newspapers.

"What was your father's name?"

"Oskar. He was my mother's first husband. She remarried. Dieter had a different father."

Ellis Jones looked at Dicks, scratching his head.

"Do you remember your times with Adolf Hitler in Munich and Landsberg prison?"

"No."

"You were with him in Munich during those exciting times."

Z remained silent.

"You remember the prison at Landsberg?"

"I don't remember."

Z shivered uncontrollably with tremors in his arms. He groaned.

"What troubles you?"

"*Magenschmerzen!* Stomach pain. Water, please."

"You will soon have water. Do you remember your mother, Klara?" Dicks asked.

"No."

"Do you remember the name of your son?"

"No."

"What about your wife, Ilse?"

"I have a letter from her."

"You remember your good friend Karl Haushofer?"

"No."

"Willi Messerschmitt, perhaps?"

"No. My stomach hurts. *Oh mein Gott!*"

Ellis Jones took over the questioning.

"You were in Alexandria as a little boy. Do you remember Egypt?"

"I don't know, I don't know," cried Z in pain.

"But Ilse you know?"

"I don't know."

"Keep talking. It will help."

Z groaned helplessly.

"Water, water. I need water."

"Why do you torture yourself?"

"Water, please water."

"Tell us why you are in pain. Speak, we want to help."

Further groans came from Z.

"Do you remember your father taking you to school, your trips to Sicily, your visits to the circus?"

"No. Water, please."

Dicks took over the questioning.

"And what about your military service in Romania?"

"I don't know."

"You remember Dr Ferdinand Sauerbruch, the great surgeon, who operated on your wounds? You remember the wounds?"

Z said nothing, but his eyes dilated with a gleam of recognition. Sauerbruch was the celebrated pioneer of thoracic surgery and Hess' brother Alfred had told Dicks before the war that the great surgeon had operated on Rudolf.

"So you remember Sauerbruch and your wounds?

"I don't know."

"But you must remember who you are. And your wife?"

"And your wife," Z repeated the words.

The two doctors looked at each other in frustration as Z started to wake up. His eyelids fluttered, and then he opened his eyes.

"I am so thirsty, so hungry," Z declared as he sat up.

Forty-four

"The treatment went well," Major Ellis Jones said. "We now know that your memory is intact. It's just that you are having trouble accessing it."

Dr Dicks and Ellis Jones were visiting Z, who was eating buttered toast and drinking a glass of milk on the verandah.

"You were able to remember quite a number of things, Herr Hess," said Dicks.

"Well, thank you gentlemen, but my mind seems to be just as empty as before."

"It will take several injections to completely restore your memory," Ellis Jones added.

"I don't think I want to go through all that again."

"It would be worth it, sir. What will your family think if you can't remember even basic things?" Dicks asked.

Z looked at the two medical men whose reputations were on the line, pleading with him to submit to another drug treatment.

"Gentlemen, I have already allowed too many foreign substances into my body. I think complete rest and fresh air will do the trick."

Dicks raised his eyebrows in frustration, having lost the battle to treat the famous patient. His hopes for a scientific paper on the subject were crushed.

Lt Malone and Z in rain gear approached the railway bridge, walking the two greyhounds Nimrod and Noah. They were followed by Lt Fenton with his Sten gun. Malone led the way pulled along by the dogs.

Nearby on the road, there were the ubiquitous wartime signs: *Food, shells and fuel must come first* over a picture of packed rail cars and another *Is your journey really necessary?* over a picture of a soldier standing in front of a ticket counter.

Z stopped to watch a locomotive pulling hundreds of rail cars slip under the bridge. He looked down at the flatbed cars whizzing past with WD (War Department) printed on their grey tarps.

"Come on, sir, it's going to rain," Malone yelled from the far end of the bridge.

Z started towards Malone, trying to restrain the dogs.

"You all right, sir?"

"Yes, Lieutenant," Z said, distracted by the heavy traffic in the rail yard.

In the nearby park, Malone and Z did a quick circular turn with the dogs before heading back under threat of a downpour just as Lt Fenton arrived.

"It seems that the Foreign Office chaps have got their knickers in a twist after reading Colonel Rees' report," Major Foley said. "I think you know what I'm referring to, Doctor."

Dr Dicks and Major Foley were walking around the Maindiff Hospital grounds.

"Of course I do, Major," Dicks said. "The Foreign Office

wants medical confirmation that Hess is fit to be tried in a court of law. Colonel Rees thinks he is mentally ill and suffers from hysterical amnesia. My job is not to cure him of his mental illness, but to restore his failing memory."

"I understand. I thought I would come by and go over the results of the narco-analysis with you."

"I'm sorry you had to come all the way out here, Major. I could have mailed you my notes."

"That's alright. It's my job to keep an eye on the man."

"Our tests confirm that the memory loss is real. Both Ellis Jones and myself witnessed it," Dicks said with pride.

"What did Hess actually say?" Foley asked.

"He didn't say that much."

"He must have given you something."

"He told us about a birthday party for his brother, Dieter. It was the usual kind of invention you get from patients under the anaesthetic."

"So this was spontaneous rambling or the result of direct questioning?"

"It was his reply to my lead question to get him talking. It is standard procedure with narco-analysis. You need to calm the patient with familiar thoughts."

"Go on."

"He talked about Dieter and his friend Franz Bieber at a birthday party, singing Nazi songs and looking smart in their military uniforms. He may have made this up."

"Dieter?"

"Yes, Dieter may be a close school friend of his. Alfred is the brother, of course. I met him before the war, you know, and there was never any mention of a Dieter. He doesn't seem to remember Alfred at all. Ellis Jones and I are trying to convince him to seek further treatment."

"I would like to see the transcript, if you don't mind."

"Of course. Look Major, I have seen the man under the anaesthetic. He can't remember the most basic things. We can only hope that he regains his memory or he won't be fit for a trial."

On the verandah, a black cat entered the room and started sniffing around as Lt Malone and Z played chess.

"Your move, sir."

Z noticed the cat rubbing up against his leg.

"How did that animal get in here?" Z asked. "That cat is the devil."

The cat ambled away, heading for the door.

"I doubt it, sir. That's Bronwen's cat from the kitchen. Where I come from, black cats are a sign of good luck."

"Not in Germany, Lieutenant. My mother used to say that black is associated with the planet Saturn and the devil. In Germany, a black cat crossing your path from right to left is a very bad sign."

"Are you kidding me, sir?"

"No, Lieutenant. It's true."

"What if the cat crosses your path from left to right?"

"Aha! That's a good sign. The cat is granting you favourable times."

"Check. Your king is in danger, sir. I think that cat just crossed your path."

Malone laughed, but Z just looked bored. He was not at all happy to be losing to an inferior player like Malone.

"I'm rather tired, Lieutenant. Can we continue the game later?"

"Of course, sir."

Forty-five

London 1944

In a miserable bedsit, Cummings shared a meal of beans and sausages with a German double agent and his burly MI5 warder named Robert. The German, whose code name was 'Pinkie' inspired by his known communist sympathies, ate ravenously. In between bites, the men washed down the greasy food with large whiskies.

Cummings put down his glass and placed a thin folder in front of the German.

"Here's the file on the Estonian officer," Cummings said.

"Good."

Pinkie opened the file and started to read.

"Don't worry, sir. We gonna be a big success tonight," Pinkie said.

"We're calling him Duchess," Cummings said.

"Duchess has a grudge against the Russians 'cause they killed his family. Sounds good, sir."

A knock on the door was heard. Robert got up to open the door for the visitor, a MI5 radio operator, by the name of Tim.

"Hello, Tim. Right on time," Cummings said.

"Paul, good to see you."

Tim stepped over to the wireless radio in the corner and started to set up.

"Cup of tea, Tim?" Robert asked.

"Please."

Robert went to the stove to pour the tea.

"So my message is that I recruited this Estonian radio operator who needs money and a new set. Right?"

"Yes. Here is the encryption."

Pinkie looked at the sheet. He took a fountain pen and put breaks in the encrypted message. Cummings looked at his watch.

"We're good. Five minutes to go, Tim?"

"Righto. Same signature?" Tim asked.

"Yes, same signature."

Pinkie stood up and stretched before sitting down at the radio with the encrypted message.

"I am getting fat, sir. I need to get out more."

Tim signalled to Cummings.

"Ready, sir?"

Cummings nodded, and Pinkie started transmitting, tapping out the encrypted message on the key.

Bristol 1944

At Whitchurch airport, a Spanish journalist named Lopez with a large moustache was seen descending from a BOAC airplane from Lisbon late at night. An MI5 agent at the terminal spotted Lopez and picked up the telephone to make a call. Lopez exited the terminal and caught a taxi to the city centre, followed by the MI5 agent in a Wolseley sedan.

It was well after midnight when Lopez arrived at his hotel.

He entered with two suitcases and went to the front desk. A clerk was busy writing in the reservations book and paid him no attention.

"I have a reservation, sir."

The man looking up at the Spanish guest was none other than Paul Cummings in a smart suit and glasses.

"You are?" Cummings asked.

"Lopez."

Cummings checked the register.

"Yes, sir. Room 321. Here are your keys, Senor Lopez. I will have our man carry your bags upstairs."

"Thank you."

Cummings rang for the bellhop, then looked down at the heavy briefcase that Lopez was holding in both hands.

"Sir, would you like us to put your bag in safekeeping? No extra charge."

Cummings turned to show Lopez the office safe just off the front desk.

"I can lock it up for you. You can pick it up in the morning."

"It's really not necessary. Thank you," Lopez replied.

The bellhop arrived to collect the bags.

"There you go. The bar is still open. Would you like some feminine company, sir?"

"I will go to my room first. Thank you."

"Tell the barman if you need anything. Good night, sir."

Lopez left with a young bellhop carrying his two suitcases. As soon as the door to the elevator closed, Cummings called a number.

"He's going to his room."

Cummings listened and waited.

"No, he took it with him. He has a typewriter."

Cummings settled back to wait. It was only a matter of

minutes before Lopez came back down and headed to the bar. Cummings picked up the phone again and called a number.

"He just entered the bar."

On the third floor, an MI5 agent used a hotel passkey to enter Lopez's room and collect the briefcase. Their information was that Lopez always carried a typewriter, and the weight of the briefcase confirmed it. The agent carried the briefcase to a room across the hall. A copy stand was already set up and a photographer and his assistant watched as the agent picked the lock on the briefcase. Inside, he found a Remington portable typewriter, a document file, and a leather-bound journal. He handed the file and the journal over to the assistant and turned his attention to the typewriter ribbon, removing it from the machine and replacing it with a new one.

The photographer adjusted the lights on the copy stand and started taking pictures as the assistant carefully turned the pages of the documents.

The agent returned to Lopez's room and picked the locks on the suitcases. He opened both of them and ran his hands around under the clothing, looking for anything out of the ordinary. In the second case, he found Lopez's wash bag and examined it carefully, pulling out a tube of toothpaste and shaving cream, a razor, moustache wax and several hair brushes. He put these items aside and ran his finger around the sides. After a moment, he pulled out a silver money clip containing a large number of ten-pound notes.

"Hello, sir. Would you like some company?" an attractive young woman asked Lopez, smiling flirtatiously.

The Spanish gentleman was sitting at the bar drinking whisky as he read the *Bristol Evening Post* newspaper. He looked up at the woman and shook his head.

"Are you sure? It is a cold night."

"Yes, miss. Thank you."

Lopez ignored the woman who remained at the bar, chatting with the barman. He finished his whisky and headed towards the lobby.

"Thanks, sir. We'll try to stall him," the MI5 agent hung up the phone in the hotel room. He turned to watch the photographer clicking away page by page.

"OK, boys. We've got to move it. He's on his way up."

The photographer and his assistant finished the last document in a hurry and then carefully slipped the document file and the journal back into the briefcase along with the typewriter. The agent grabbed the briefcase and opened Lopez's door as the photographer raced toward the lift, running into the Spaniard in hallway.

"Hello, sir. Is the bar still open? Would you know?" asked the photographer, putting his arm up to slow Lopez down.

"I was just in the bar, sir. It is still open, I think."

"Well, thank you. I believe you have an accent, sir."

"Yes, I'm Spanish."

"You lucky devil, you. Out of the bloody war and all that. Well, sir. Thank you and have a good night."

The photographer let Lopez go and took the lift down. In the lobby, he gave a thumbs up to Cummings.

"Good work. Let's move out. I'll inform the staff."

"Give us ten minutes, sir."

Forty-six

London 1944

"The mail is on your desk, sir," the secretary said. "There is a letter from Abergavenny. You said you wanted to know when it arrived."

Major Foley had just arrived at MI6 headquarters when he ran into his secretary.

"Thanks, Mary."

Foley removed his hat and coat. He lit a cigarette standing near the window looking out at a bombed-out building being razed by a bulldozer. He returned to his desk, sat down, and opened the letter from Abergavenny. He pulled out a typed document and started to read.

In a London suburb, Cummings, Claudia and Werner sat in a car watching for a no. 11 bus. A moment later, a red double-decker bus turned the corner and pulled over at the bus stop across the street.

'There it is. You better go now," Cummings said.

Werner and Claudia got out and headed for the bus. Pinkie was already on board, sitting downstairs near the front, but they ignored him as they climbed on and sat together on seats with a view of both the front and the back of the bus. The bus pulled out and Cummings followed in the car.

The bus followed its usual route through dusty bombed-out sections of the city. The Spanish journalist Lopez got on at one of the stops, but stayed at the back of the bus near the stairs going up to the top. He looked for his contact inside and easily identified Pinkie in a dark suit with a red tie and a white carnation in the buttonhole at the front.

Werner and Claudia watched as Pinkie stood up and walked slowly back to Lopez. Werner pulled a German Leica camera with a wide-angle lens from his pocket, and hiding it under his coat, took a picture of Lopez just as he slipped Pinkie a newspaper containing a brown envelope in the doorway. Lopez came inside and took seat as Pinkie got off the bus.

Lopez continued on for several stops before leaving the bus, followed by Werner and Claudia. Across the street, Cummings waited in the car as Werner and Claudia approached.

"He's going to his flat," Cummings said to Claudia and Werner as they arrived at the car.

"Who is this Lopez, Paul?" Claudia asked.

"He is the London journalist of a well-known Spanish newspaper, but on the side, he runs a lucrative spy network in Madrid, and feeds information to the Germans. He just paid £500 of Abwehr money to Pinkie."

"We have bugged his flat," Werner added. "Lopez has a Russian sweetheart who we hear from time to time."

"Nothing obscene, I hope," Claudia inquired with a laugh.

"We get it all, Claudia. What did you think?" Werner replied with a grin.

In their row house in Islington, Cummings and Claudia made love in their small bedroom. Steffi was asleep next door and the only sound in the house was the noise of an ambulance and the distant sound of an AA gun on the outskirts of the city. The bedside lamp came on briefly as Claudia went to have a look at Steffi. Moments later, she returned to bed.

"When did they break Pinkie?" Claudia asked.

"Last year," Paul replied.

"And now he is working for us."

"Yes. He is quite good. We have invented a new contact for Pinkie. This new fellow is a pro-Nazi, Estonian radio operator named Duchess."

Claudia cuddled up to her husband, who massaged her back.

"So Pinkie reports to the Abwehr in Madrid," Claudia said. "And of course, these reports are full of absolute rubbish created by our services."

"It is not all rubbish, you know. That would be too easy to spot. I hear it is quite a job creating this stuff out of thin air. The trick is to hide the lie among real facts of no military significance," Cummings replied.

"I was thinking to myself why haven't we used Max as a double? He has contacts in the SS. He is famous. He is not some obscure agent in the field. He could be useful."

"He's out of bounds, the PM's instructions, Claudia."

"I know that. But it might help his case if he collaborated a bit in the war effort. The Russians want to hang him. He could be a double agent like Pinkie."

Cummings was silent for a while.

"He is your friend, *Liebling*. You can help him."

"I am not sure what he can do, but it might be worthwhile bringing it up with the major."

"Dieter is Dieter Gunther, not Dieter Hörner," Major Foley said to Cummings as they walked along the Thames Embankment. "He was recruited by the SS and killed in France in May 1940."

Cummings and the major were trailing behind Claudia and Steffi, who had stopped to look down at the river boats.

"We think Franz Bieber is with the SD, the *Sicherheitsdienst*," Foley added.

"Well, that is very interesting," Cummings said.

"What worries us is that if Bieber works for their foreign intelligence service, the *Ausland SD* section, he would know about Max's recruitment by the SS."

"So Major, you think that Bieber may be working with Max?"

"Max belongs to Himmler and the SS, so clearly the *Ausland SD* section is involved. Remember, Bieber has a special relationship with the family."

"So Bieber may be involved somehow in Max's story?"

"Absolutely. They would certainly use him as a resource," Foley said.

"You think that Max may have the means to communicate with Bieber?"

"Of course, anything is possible."

"We could use Max to communicate with Bieber. Claudia was suggesting the very same thing the other night."

"It's an idea worth exploring."

"Feed Bieber and the SD with misinformation."

Forty-seven

Abergavenny 1944

In the night, Z tossed and turned in his bed in the Maindiff prisoner's wing. He got up and went to the window, looking out at the moonlit sky. Z heard the muffled voice of Herr Oberst.

"*Sie sind auf feindlichem Gebiet, Soldat.* You are in enemy territory. You saw the trains at the station?"

"Yes, the train with the WD sign, Herr Oberst. I think it means War Department."

"*Sehr wahrscheinlich, Soldat.* Very likely, bombs for Germany. God be with us."

"Herr Oberst. What are your orders?"

"Destroy the track, soldier. Stop the train. That is your mission."

Z looked briefly unnerved by the order as Herr Oberst's voice faded away. He put on his shoes and dressed in a pullover and a grey coat. He climbed onto the window sill and slipped out through a hole in the wire mesh.

It was very dark and noisy in the marshalling yard at the

Abergavenny railway station. A crew of welders was working on a rail car late into the night. A locomotive rolled by, pulling cars with WD tarps.

Z sneaked around the yard and then headed south. He ran into some bushes as a signalman appeared in the distance, coming his way with a lantern.

In the morning, Bronwen wearing an apron, stopped by Z's room with a breakfast tray.

"Mr Hess, your breakfast is served. I'm putting it on the table."

Bronwen was surprised by the silence.

"Mr Hess. Time to get up, sir."

Bronwen looked perplexed by the silent room.

"Mr Hess. Your breakfast is served."

Z awakened on a cot in a Nissen hut near the railroad tracks. He stretched and stood up. He stepped toward a window covered in coal dust and looked out at the tracks in the early morning light. He jumped at the sound of a man snoring loudly on a cot at the back of the hut and slipped out the door as fast as he could. Outside, he headed south again along the tracks away from the station.

Several hours later, Z approached the Usk River and tried to cross to the other side. He removed his shoes and socks, and started across, slipping and sliding, and fell on his arse in the deeper portion of the river. Dripping wet, he stumbled out of the river on the other side and hid himself in a copse of trees. He removed his wet pants and hung them up to dry on a stone wall in the warm sunshine. He sat down in the long grass and soon was fast asleep.

"He disappeared during the night, sir," Dr Dicks said. "Lt Malone thinks he climbed through a hole in the wire mesh enclosure."

Dr Dicks was on the phone in the hospital office while Lt Malone stood by. Dicks hung up and looked at Malone.

"Major Foley said he would call back in an hour. He is sending Cummings to give us a hand."

"We can organize a search party, sir. He can't have gone far. He has no money."

"The major wants to keep it under wraps. It won't look good in the press if we have a Nazi prisoner on the loose in town."

"Let's retrace your steps when you walk the dogs," Cummings suggested to Malone as they drove slowly along a street in a military staff car near the Maindiff hospital.

"With the dogs, we usually go over the railway bridge to the park," Malone said as he turned onto the bridge.

"Pull over here a moment, will you?"

Malone stopped the car in the middle of the bridge and Cummings climbed out, looking down at the railway tracks.

"We often come this way, sir."

"I didn't realise this was such a busy junction," Cummings said as he looked down at the rail yard.

Cummings put field glasses to his eyes and took a long look at the sheds along the tracks as Malone waved on a lorry stuck behind them.

"All the traffic south to Newton Abbot and Weymouth goes

this way, sir," Malone said.

"He could try to catch a freight going south from here," Cummings said.

"There are guards in the yard and work going on at all hours of the day and night, sir. He would have to jump on a moving train. I doubt he could catch a stopped train in the yard without being seen," Malone replied.

"Let's take a look at the park."

They returned to the car. Malone and Cummings drove off the bridge and around the nearby park. They stopped the car and looked around, but saw no sign of the fugitive.

Z made his way south, walking along the Usk riverbank. From time to time, he stopped to search for berries in the bushes along the shore.

After an hour or two, Z returned to the railway tracks and headed south again. He noticed a farmhouse on the brow of a hill and headed towards it. It was a large and prosperous-looking farm. He climbed over a stone wall and crossed a field into the Penperlleni farm. Z collected a shovel near a barn and started to dig in the vegetable garden.

Three land girls in dungarees were working in a shed near the barn packing farm produce for market. They noticed Z in the vegetable garden, digging up carrots and stuffing them in his pockets.

A middle-aged farm woman soon appeared near the main house and shouted at Z. He stuffed a carrot hungrily in his mouth as the woman approached.

Cummings and Malone walked along the tracks at the

railway station. Nearby stood the Nissen shed where Z had slept during the night.

"What do you think, sir?"

"I think he walked out following the tracks. It is the easiest way to leave town without anyone seeing him. I think he went south. To go north would be risky because he would need to get around the station without being observed."

"I agree, sir. He has to be headed south."

Cummings and Malone returned to the car.

"Let's look at where he might have gone," Cummings said as Malone pulled out a topographic map of the region from a desk drawer at the Maindiff hospital office.

"Here's the railway going south, sir. He could make it on foot to Newport in a day. It's an easy walk, a distance of about 20 miles," Malone said, drawing his finger along the route.

"Good point, Lieutenant."

Dr Dicks entered the room and saw the two men looking at the map.

"He's been gone for almost a day," Dicks said. "He could be on his way to the continent by now if he jumped a freight last night and caught a ship out of Cardiff, Bristol or Weymouth?"

"I am not so sure, Doctor. We looked at the rail yard and it would not be easy to jump on a moving train during the night. There is a good deal of surveillance at the yard. We think he walked out."

"Walked out? Why not take a bus?"

"His face would give him away," Cummings said.

"Anybody sees his mug, they are going to call the police," Malone added.

"You know he wanted Colonel Rees to send him home on

that Swedish hospital ship," Dicks said.

"I didn't know that," Cummings said. "So you think he wants to leave and return to Germany?"

"A neutral country like Spain would be a good choice or in a pinch France or Belgium," Dicks said. "I don't think he would dare return to Germany."

"I"m not so sure, Doctor. This may just be a lark and he wants a break from captivity. To get out and feel free again."

"Where would he go, sir?" Malone asked.

"I think he would keep walking south on the tracks until he got hungry. He knows we are looking for him, so he is going to avoid the roads."

Forty-eight

Cummings and Malone went from farm to farm in the staff car, turning left, turning right, stopping to hail farm labourers on the road. At one point they stopped the car and climbed to a promontory overlooking the railway tracks, but there was no sign of Z anywhere.

After hours of driving around the Brecon Hills, they turned a corner and noticed several people gathered in a garden behind a thatched cottage in the village of Penperlleni. They pulled over and got out.

Z was eating a large bowl of soup surrounded by three young, rosy-cheeked land girls. Nearby, an older woman was cooking the evening meal on an open-hearth fireplace. Z looked up and waved as Cummings and Malone walked into the garden.

"We found your friend tramping around our vegetable patch," the woman told them.

"Did you now? Well, thank you for looking after him," Cummings said.

"I'm Elizabeth Wynne, these are Janie, Fanny and Doreen."

The women waved at the two handsome newcomers.

"I am Captain Paul Cummings and this is Lt Malone."

The land girls smiled flirtatiously at Cummings and Malone,

laughing nervously.

"I found your friend digging up carrots in the garden, so I invited him to dine with us," Mrs Wynne said.

"Frau Wynne has a wonderful farm," Z said. "And these ladies are doing such hard work."

The land girls smiled at him.

"Mr Hess had a farm in Germany, so he is very interested in our work. Would you like some soup?"

The two men looked famished and nodded their assent.

"Mr Hess was just telling us about a state dinner with Herr Hitler, Göring and company at the *Reichskanzler's* house in Berlin. It is fascinating, isn't it, girls?"

"I am sure it is," Cummings said with a cynical air.

Mrs Wynne indicated two chairs for Cummings and Malone, who joined the women at the table.

As the sun faded in the west, Z ran his hand through the golden oats on the perimeter of the farm overlooking the Usk River valley. He examined a handful of oats with an experienced eye before showing the grain to Cummings.

"See these oats, Captain. Germany will never succeed in starving the British Isles if you have such wonderful grain. This is very good land. Oats can be difficult to grow, too many *Schädlinge*, you know?"

"Yes, we call them pests."

"I like Wales. The land is fertile. You can hear the wind blowing off the fields. It is like my home back in Germany."

"You don't have a home anymore, Max. Get that into your head. You can never go back to Germany."

"I know, Captain."

"I might be able to get you a job on a farm just like this.

Would you like that?"

"You can get me a job on a farm like this?" Z asked.

"It is possible. Write a confession. Tell the authorities you were coerced into playing Rudolf Hess and I can plead your case, Max."

"Who do I have to write to?"

"Write to Lord Simon or the PM. You can do it. Tell them everything you know."

Cummings, with a wistful air, looked down at the river. He turned slowly towards Z.

"Max, you can't go running off any time you like. It just won't do."

Z brushed the grain from his fingers.

"Yes, I know, Captain," Z said with sadness. "It was great fun to get out and walk this land. Breathe the air and feel free. This is a magical place."

"Yes, it is quite lovely, Max, but we better go. I have to catch a train for London."

Forty-nine

London 1944

"Mr Lopez, you were arrested yesterday at Bristol airport trying to flee the country," Lt-Colonel Stephens said.

The Spanish journalist Lopez was standing in the middle of the interrogation room at Latchmere House being questioned by Stephens in the company of Captain Short.

"I was not fleeing the country, sir. I am a Spanish citizen and journalist. I can come and go as I please," Lopez said, looking very tired and frightened.

"You have declared that you were an 'unwilling intermediary' in the Angel Alcazar espionage ring."

"I do not know any espionage ring, sir. I was just doing favours for old friends."

"You were seen giving money to a German agent in this country. I have the photograph here to prove it."

Lopez looked at the black-and-white photograph held up by Stephens showing Lopez handing Pinkie a newspaper at the back of a double-decker bus.

"This looks very much like espionage to me, sir."

Lopez said nothing.

"If you are giving money to a friend, you would do it

openly, would you not? This is not the behaviour of people above reproach. This is the behaviour of criminals and spies, Mr Lopez."

Lopez looked away.

"I believe you work for several Spanish and Argentine newspapers?"

"Yes."

"You are paid each month for your work. Am I right?"

"Yes, sir. The payment is monthly by bank draft."

"Bank draft? So please tell me how you happen to have £1,000 in your pocket," Stephens asked with a cynical air.

Lopez said nothing.

"Are these funds for other German spies, Mr Lopez? Or are these funds for yourself?"

At home, Cummings poured himself a whisky while Claudia prepared the evening meal in the kitchen. Steffi played on the floor with a wooden toy.

"They arrested Lopez, the Spanish journalist," Cummings said.

"What will happen to him?"

"Aiding and abetting the enemy on British soil. I would expect some prison time."

"That means that Pinkie is burned, Paul. The Germans will expect Pinkie to be arrested after Lopez."

"The government wants to make a show of closing down the Alcazar network. They are feeding intelligence to the Germans and the Japanese. I can't believe the director Guy Liddell would support such a move. Masterman is calling it a disaster."

Claudia stirred the pot on the stove.

"By cutting off the head, they think they can stop it," Cummings said. "Our whole double-cross system could come tumbling down. Pinkie, Duke, Duchess, Flake, all of them."

"The German controllers will watch the traffic," Claudia replied. "They will scrutinize everything. They hate to lose agents. They will want to believe in their agent's integrity, you know."

"So you think we can write another narrative?"

"Of course we can. MI5 looked for Pinkie, but was unable to find him. Pinkie moved away. He got a new job. He fought with a girlfriend and got thrown out of his flat."

"Pinkie got thrown out of his flat?" Steffi intoned, laughing as she played on the floor. "Out the window?"

"No, dear. It's just an expression meaning put out of the flat. Not thrown out the window," Claudia said, grinning at her daughter.

"We only throw naughty girls out the window, don't we, darling?" Cummings teased his daughter, who jumped up ready to run away from her dad.

"So, Miss Roth, you were the one who received the Hess letters?" Major Foley asked the young bespectacled woman in a WRNS uniform sitting in his office at MI6 Headquarters.

Miss Lena Roth, with an ample bosom and outrageous red lipstick, was an Austrian immigrant and spoke English with a noticeable Scottish accent. She flirted openly with the aging major.

"Yes, sir. I work in Dilly Knox's hut 16 at Bletchley. It's mostly Abwehr traffic - German codes and such, like," Lena Roth said, smiling. "They call us Dilly's fillies, sir."

"Dilly's fillies?" Foley laughed.

"I am a cryptanalyst, sir. We work three shifts in hut 16. I caught your letter in the wee hours. It didn't take long, a common alphanumeric code, you know."

"There were secret messages in those letters?"

"Yes, sir."

The major stood up with serious concern on his face.

"Just a minute, Miss Roth."

He rushed out of the office to talk to his secretary.

"Call Felix. Get Guy Liddell and Paul Cummings on the phone. It's urgent."

Foley returned to his office just as Miss Roth crossed her shapely legs in such a way that the major had a good view.

"How many letters, Miss Roth?" Foley demanded.

"All of them, sir. Same signature, same alphanumeric code," Miss Roth said candidly.

"Who knows this?"

"No one, sir. Just you. We are held to the highest standards of confidentiality," the woman said with some pride.

Fifty

"Hello, Paul. Thanks for coming on such short notice," Major Foley said.

"That's fine, sir."

In the failing light, Foley gestured toward a chair near the covered bar in the yard of the safe house. Cummings sat down while the major fiddled with his pipe. Music from inside the house drifted across the yard.

"I had a talk with your director Guy Liddell," Foley said. "A situation has occurred. Our Max has been communicating with his German handlers."

Cummings was stunned.

"How?" he asked finally. "How is that possible?"

"We talked about Bieber working in the *Ausland SD* section. Well, Max has been communicating with him in code."

"Bloody hell. I can't believe it."

"Well, believe it. I want you to return to Wales as soon as possible. He is being taken to the Mardy POW camp tonight, where he will be held in solitary until we get things sorted out."

"Of course, sir. I will catch the first train in the morning," Cummings said.

"I know you have developed a close relationship with the

man, Paul," Foley said, "but he has been lying to you. It's time to use that relationship to get to the bottom of this. We have no idea how much damage he has done, if any. It is not like he is free to roam about the country noting troop movements."

Abergavenny 1944

In the early morning hours, two British soldiers hauled Z in shackles down the stairs of the Maindiff Hospital into a waiting paddy wagon. They threw him roughly into the back and slammed the door, driving off into the night.

At the Mardy camp, Z was pulled from the van and hustled into a wire enclosure in the yard. A soldier entered the cage and started to systematically beat him with a billy club. Z cried out but the blows kept coming.

The following afternoon Cummings arrived at the Mardy camp in a staff car driven by Lt Malone. Cummings headed towards the office, leaving Malone with the car.

"Hello, Agent Cummings," Davies said cynically as Cummings entered his office. "I understand you're not with the Scots Guards at all, but a spook working for MI5."

"We all have a job to do, Colonel," Cummings replied.

"Yes, of course. It looks like your Major Foley has his knickers in a right twist."

"I need to see our man."

"We made the arrest as requested. They said to make it rough so my chaps may have left some marks."

Cummings frowned upon hearing this.

"Well, I will take it from here, sir," Cummings said.

"Yes, you will," Davies said, "and you will have to take him with you."

Cummings stared at him, uncomprehending.

"You can't leave that Nazi tosser here," Davies said. "I can't protect him. Everybody wants to shank the bastard."

Helmut walked Cummings over to the enclosed cage in the middle of the camp. Inside, Z sat uncomfortably on a bench wrapped in a blanket. He had cuts and bruises on his face.

"*Stehen Sie auf,*" Helmut ordered.

Z stood up slowly, looking exhausted and frightened.

"Call me when you have finished, sir."

Cummings waved to Helmut and turned his attention to the prisoner.

"Hello, Max. It appears that you have been rather naughty."

"Captain, I have done nothing. These two brutes came for me yesterday."

"Foley's people are not very happy with you and for good reason. You abused our friendship, Max. You lied to me."

"Pardon?"

"You lied to me about Dieter. Your brother Dieter Gunther was in the SS. You had different fathers. That's why the name didn't pop out at us. He sold you to Herr Oberst, didn't he?"

"*Macht nichts.*"

"Your brother had plans for you. He and Franz Bieber. Didn't they?"

Z looked surprised.

"Bieber was just a boy from our village, a friend of my brother."

"You remember Dieter's birthday party, Max. Dieter and Franz were in their black SS uniforms. Foley's people made the connection. Dieter was Waffen SS, but Franz was with the foreign intelligence service, the *Ausland SD* of the *Sicherheitsdienst*. A cipher analyst, Max. Why don't you tell me the rest?"

Z sighed. When he spoke, he spoke in a whisper.

"In school, I was always top of my class," he said wistfully, "but Dieter was my mother's favourite. It didn't matter what I did. Mother always preferred my brother. She would go on and on how Dieter did this, Dieter did that."

"When he was killed in France, mother became very depressed. She abandoned the farm and returned to Rostock to look after my grandmother. When Herr Oberst found me on the farm, I was living hand to mouth, trying to survive by bringing in the potato crop."

Z watched the prisoners in the recreation area milling about, trying to keep warm as they sneaked looks at Cummings.

"I was happy because I was eating three meals a day and I had a goal. I had a mission from the Führer. I was not free, but I was an important man working for the SS. The teachers thought I was a quick learner."

"You were trained to use alphanumeric codes? You didn't tell me that, Max. You held that back. You used secret code to write to your people in Germany."

"I was trained in lots of things, Captain, including writing secret code. Franz started me with simple codes, Caesar ciphers, alphabet codes, that sort of thing. Then with more sophisticated codes. I was trained to send messages through ordinary letter writing."

"We had our people look at a couple of your letters. What have you done, Max?"

"I was to observe German bomber raids over London, troop strength, and aircraft production. I was not free in my movements, so I wasn't able to report much."

"You need to tell me everything, Max. I need to know about every letter you used to convey vital information and where it went."

"Am I to stay here?"

"I don't know, Max, that depends on you. If you agree to work for us and not against us, then perhaps we can continue to accommodate you at Maindiff."

"You can't leave me here, Captain. They will kill me."

"I took you into my house, Max. You ate with my family under my roof and you never told me you were working for Bieber."

"I'm sorry."

"If you return, you will work for us. We will give you all the information you need to send along to your German contacts. You will be a double agent working against your friends in Germany."

Z suddenly realized the price he would have to pay to leave the POW camp.

Fifty-one

Evesham 1944

A military staff car pulled up in front of Wood Norton Hall, one of the oldest Victorian homes in England and the temporary home of the BBC foreign service during the war. As Lt Malone and Lt Fenton stepped out of the car, Cummings appeared in the doorway of the building and came over to greet them.

"Did you have a good trip?"

"Yes, sir. It's not such a long drive," Malone replied.

Cummings leaned into the car to get a look at Z in the back seat.

"How are you keeping, Mr Hess?"

"Captain, they say I will be making a declaration on the radio. This can't be true."

"Yes, I heard that. I don't know what this is all about. Lord Simon is here to explain."

Z climbed out of the car and looked up at the extravagant facade.

"*Ich kann diesen Text nicht lesen.* I can't read this, Lord

Simon," Z said to Lord Simon and Major Foley in the studio, just as Cummings returned to the soundproofed room.

They should have waited for me, Cummings thought. He had been called away by an urgent phone call and had returned to find Z already standing at a microphone with a typed manuscript surrounded by several sound technicians.

"This is a wonderful opportunity, Herr Hess," Lord Simon said, "for you to talk directly to the German people. If it is conclusive, we may require your services on a regular basis."

"I cannot say these words, sir," Z said. "It says I will be returning to Germany. I don't want to go back."

"Don't worry, Max," Cummings whispered as he stepped closer, "this is just a test recording. We would never send you back to an execution. These gentlemen simply want to hear your voice."

Z relaxed somewhat, seeing Cummings in the studio. Lord Simon took the cue from Cummings.

"You are perhaps the greatest peacemaker of our time," he said, "so we want you to tell the German people to lay down their arms. Continuing to fight will only lead to unmitigated disaster. Can you do that?"

"I will try, sir."

"If it doesn't pass muster, we can always start over."

A sound technician appeared in the doorway and gave the signal to start the recording. The Nazi party anthem (the Horst Wessel song) played in the background.

"*Meine deutschen Kamaraden. Ich bin Ihr Reichsminister, Herr Rudolf Hess.* I flew to Scotland in 1941 for a peace meeting with the British government. These meetings produced nothing. Now, after four years of conflict, it is time to consider putting an end to this terrible war."

Z's voice took on a deep resonance filling the room as he

gained confidence in the words. Lord Simon nodded his approbation and Cummings gave him a thumbs up.

"Every day Allied forces bomb our beloved German cities, now reduced to ruin. After the loss of millions of young men on the Russian and Italian fronts, and in North Africa, it is time for a peace settlement. I have met secretly with Herr Himmler in Zurich, and together we have decided to seize power in Germany. Herr Hitler, Göring, Goebbels, and all the Nazi warmongers must go. I intend to fly into Augsburg in a week's time and from there we will march together on the Bavarian capital of Munich with white flags where I will deliver a speech to the German nation."

Major Foley whispered his praise for the speech to Lord Simon, who glanced sharply at him and put a finger to his lips.

"I am appealing to all senior German officers in the armed forces to permit the men under their command to leave their posts and to return to their families. We are asking all German forces to lay down their arms and go home. In two weeks time, the peace negotiations will begin and we will put an end to this terrible war."

Z turned the page.

"*Ich bin Rudolf Hess. Rudolf Hess aber ist Deutschland wie Deutschland Rudolf Hess ist. Es ist Zeit, um den neuen Frieden zu feiern! Seligen Frieden. Grüße den Frieden! Grüße den Frieden!* (I am Rudolf Hess, Rudolf Hess is Germany, as Germany is Rudolf Hess. It is time to celebrate the new peace! Blessed peace. Hail to peace.)"

Z's voice reached a crescendo with his final words and faded out with the music. Cummings, Foley and Lord Simon were astonished by his performance. A sound technician entered the room to collect the text, and to turn off the microphone.

"I am thinking of Hess' speech to the party at Nuremberg in 1934," Foley said.

"*Die Partei ist Hitler*. I remember that speech. I listened to it often," Z said.

"Yes, I am sure you did. A very great speech. Excellent work for a first read, Herr Hess. I will show it to the PM. Thank you so much for coming in," Lord Simon said as a sound technician signalled to him from the doorway.

"But none of it is true. I never met with Herr Himmler in Switzerland."

"Of course. You did very well," Lord Simon said, shaking Z's hand and leaving the room to take a call from London.

Cummings hurried Z out of the recording studio and into the courtyard. They headed towards the staff car.

"You think I did a good job, Captain?" Z asked.

"You were amazing. I think they will use that recording. It will go out on the black propaganda radio. *Soldansender Calais* or *Kurtwellensender Atlantik*."

"But it tells lies."

"But, of course, Max. That's the point of it all. It is full of false information. You have just made a friend in Lord Simon. He can help you."

"You mean I will be like Lord Haw Haw in Berlin, telling lies to the British people? But Captain, if German soldiers believe me and lay down their arms, the SS will have them killed. I know this. I read the papers. They will think this message is a joke."

"The German people are tired of war. We are tired of war. We just need them to come to their senses," Cummings said.

"So you think I did a good job," Z said.

"You did an excellent job. If you didn't have that face, you could run for a seat in parliament."

Cummings and Z laughed as they joined Lt Malone and Lt Fenton at the car.

"Goodbye, Captain," Z said, getting into the back seat.

"Goodbye, sir. Have a good trip," Cummings said as Malone started the engine and waved as they drove off.

Fifty-two

Berlin 1973

"Did they ever use that recording?" Terry asked.

Cummings was wistful for a moment as he remembered Z's extraordinary performance that day in the studio.

"Unfortunately, no. The PM decided not to use it," Cummings said. "With the Normandy invasion planned for June, it was decided to use Max for more subtle disinformation purposes. Miss Roth, the cryptanalyst from Bletchley, was sent to Abergavenny to work with him."

Cummings smiled suddenly as he remembered Miss Ross.

"I think it was Foley's idea to recruit Miss Roth to work with Max."

Abergavenny 1944

Major Foley and the elegant cryptanalyst sat with Z on the verandah at Maindiff as Cummings stood nearby.

"What is your signature, Herr Hess?" Miss Roth asked.

"Signature?"

"*Ihr Zeichen?*"

"*Die Lachlinie*. The laugh-line, you know. The squiggle at the end. I use it as a code signal."

"So you use the squiggle to indicate to the reader that you are using a code and then the grid comes from the last two words on the first line?" Roth asked.

"Yes, in this one we have 4 letters in one word and 5 in the second, so we have a 4x5 grid."

"So you put a secret code into all your letters to Ilse?" Foley asked.

"Only when I had something to say. All the letters going to Ilse are being read by the *Sicherheitsdienst*. The squiggle indicates which have secret messages."

"We have put together several coded letters for Professor Gerl and Haushofer, which need a touch-up. Let's go over them," Foley said.

Roth pulled out a typed draft letter and put it on the table. Z started to read.

"Oh, I wouldn't use this term."

"Don't worry," Foley said, "we want you to adapt the text to your own style. Isn't that right, Miss Roth?"

"Yes, it is, Major," she smiled at him, then turned to Z. "We will build the code around your changes. Remember, you are the writer and it has to be in your own terms."

"This letter tells the reader that you are now in a better position to observe war material shipments and troop movements on the south coast," Foley said, observing Z's reaction.

"Please read through it and make the changes you think are necessary, Mr Hess," Miss Roth said. "Then we will adapt it to carry the encrypted message."

"Are you going to use the railway bridge as his observation point?" Cummings asked.

"Yes, his handlers know he is in Abergavenny and will know about the rail link. So it is perfect for observing traffic going south," Foley said.

"Excellent plan," Cummings said as he thought about the upcoming invasion of France.

Abergavenny had already seen an enormous increase in rail traffic as US, British and Canadian troops were sent south and congregated near ports from Portsmouth to Land's End.

Fifty-three

Berlin 1973

"You know Max contributed to 'Operation Fortitude', the huge deception conducted by the Allies to lead the Germans to believe that they would be landing in Pas-de-Calais or in Norway, and not in Normandy," Cummings said. "Max's coded messages told his SS handlers that traffic in the Abergavenny rail yard was down due to a massive troop buildup in the southeast."

"Did Max have any idea what he was doing?" Terry asked.

"Not really. Most double agents were fed information by the Twenty Committee and had no idea how the pieces fit together. Of course, it soon became clear to him on June 6 as the Normandy landings were announced in the press."

London, Islington 1944

It was the evening of Boxing Day, and the Prince of Wales pub on McKenzie Road was crowded. A local couple had just announced their engagement and there was a noisy celebration going on.

Werner and his new wife, Louise, were having a drink with colleagues when Cummings spotted them in the crowd and waved.

"Hello, sir. You have met Louise, I think," Werner said with pride.

"Yes, I have. Hello, Louise. It is nice to see you both. Hope they are treating you well in your new job, Werner?"

"It was more fun working with you and Claudia, sir," Werner said. "Stay a while and I'll buy you a pint."

"Thanks, Werner, but I have to get home. It's getting late. Some other time, perhaps. Bye."

"Give my best to Claudia."

Cummings waved to the couple as he left the pub.

At the Islington row house, Cummings stepped into the cramped dining room with its red check tablecloth and homemade Christmas decorations with a decidedly German touch. Claudia was busy sewing the seam on a new dress with an old Singer hand-cranked sewing machine.

"Sorry, I am late. I saw Werner and Louise at the pub. They were having a grand old time."

"Werner is in love, Paul. I am so happy for him. He has had a hard life, you know. He deserves it. I put your supper on the stove."

Claudia went to the kitchen as Cummings hung up his coat and hat. As Claudia entered the kitchen, the clock on the wall struck 9:30 p.m. Suddenly there was a huge explosion in the neighbourhood and a series of jolts shook the house like an earthquake.

"What the hell was that?" Cummings asked.

Cummings ran to the front door and out on to the street as

Steffi awakened with a cry in the second-floor bedroom. Neighbours were running into the street as they tried to determine the location of the explosion. Claudia quickly climbed the stairs to comfort her daughter. After a moment, Cummings returned to the house in a state of shock.

"It's the pub on McKenzie Road. There is a huge fire burning. You can see it from the street," Cummings called to Claudia at the top of the stairs.

"Werner and Louise were in that pub, Paul. You just came from there. You are lucky to be alive."

Horrified, Cummings looked at his wife.

Fifty-four

Berlin 1973

"Where did you meet your wife, Paul?" Terry asked.

Cummings' eyes lit up as he remembered those happy, careless days before the war.

"We met in the south of France and were married in London in '38. I was working at the passport office here in Berlin at the time. Claudia and her family were from Cologne. They're Jewish and their lives started to come apart in '37. They were in hiding and had lost everything so I had the passport office issue them visas to emigrate to Britain."

Cummings looked around to see office workers and tourists filling the seats in the *biergarten* as the end of the day approached.

"So how were you recruited into the service?"

"I had worked with Frank Foley in Berlin. I read German literature at Oxford so Frank thought I would make a good intelligence officer."

"So what happened to Max after you returned to London with your family?"

"I saw him again in 1945 at Maindiff after his second suicide attempt."

NICHOLAS KINSEY

Abergavenny, February 1945

In the Maindiff Hospital kitchen, Bronwen and several kitchen workers in white aprons were preparing the midday meal as Z suddenly appeared in the doorway wearing his Luftwaffe uniform.

"Mr Hess! You are not supposed to come in here," Bronwen shouted.

"Lt Malone and Fenton are out and I need a knife for my toast."

Z went to the cutlery drawer. Bronwen started towards him but froze when he pulled out a big kitchen knife with an 8-inch blade.

"Don't worry, Bronwen," he said, "I will bring it back soon."

He was on his way out when he suddenly turned and raised his arm in the Nazi salute.

"*Heil Hitler!*"

Astonished, Bronwen and her colleagues exchanged worried looks as Z left the room. Bronwen removed her apron and decided to go for help.

She entered the Maindiff office in the prisoner's wing where she found Dr Dicks on the phone. He held up a finger to indicate that he would be with her in a moment.

Lt Malone entered the office and ran into Bronwen.

"Lieutenant," she said breathlessly, "Mr Hess has taken a knife from the kitchen!"

"When did this happen?" Malone asked.

"Just a moment ago. He's in his Luftwaffe uniform. I thought you ought to know."

"Good, you did the right thing," Malone said.

Malone rang an alarm bell signalling his need for urgent assistance before he ran down the hall to Z's quarters.

He was nearly too late. Z was sitting in an armchair with blood seeping through his shirt from a chest wound and the knife was lying on the floor. As Malone entered the room, Z in a state of shock whispered: "I tried to reach the heart, but I don't think I did, Lieutenant."

Malone was about to call for medical help when Dr Dicks and two orderlies burst into the room. Dr Dicks quickly appraised the situation.

"Lieutenant, let's get him across the hall into the clinic before he loses too much blood."

Cummings first learned of Z's suicide attempt in London. Before he could take the train, he heard news that the wound was superficial and his life was not in danger. Clearly, Z had lost his nerve and hadn't used enough pressure when he tried to stab himself.

"How are you feeling, Max?" Cummings asked.

"Hello, Captain," Z smiled, "You came here for me?"

"Of course."

Z got up from a nap on the couch dressed in pyjamas and a red scarf around his neck. As he put on a dressing gown and slid his feet into slippers, Cummings examined various notes and photographs stuck to the interior window of the verandah: a letter from Ilse, a photograph of Herr Hitler, and other memorabilia.

"Are you having a good war?" Z asked. "How is young Steffi and your wife Claudia?"

"They are doing very well, Max," Cummings said, "but I have some bad news. Werner and his wife were killed by a V2 rocket that struck a pub in Islington on Boxing Day. I was having a drink with them minutes before it happened. 68 people were killed. Claudia was deeply affected, Werner was her cousin."

"I am sorry, sir."

"It was a direct hit. You can't run for shelter from a V2. It comes in faster than the speed of sound. Werner was a devoted employee and quite brilliant. The service put on a special commemoration for him."

"He was a very nice fellow."

"Yes, he was. So I am not having a good war, Max. No one is having a good war. My brother Brian is now with a British unit in the Ardennes. You have heard about the German counterattack in the papers. Some twenty thousand American soldiers were killed in that attack and almost three times as many Germans. I am sick of the war. Everyone is sick of the damn war."

Cummings picked up one of Z's sketches and glanced at it before putting it back on the coffee table.

"We are getting our revenge now. We are destroying the German will to fight. We just firebombed Dresden, one of the most beautiful cities in Europe. It is nothing but a pile of ashes. The new incendiary bombs set a city ablaze, burning it to the ground. There is no escape for the population, Max. We may be dying in large numbers here in Britain, but the slaughter of German civilians is unprecedented. Just look at the victims of Allied fire bombings in Cologne, Dortmund, Hamburg, and Frankfurt. There is no sense to it all."

Z glanced at Cummings with a surprised look, fascinated by the man's emotional turmoil. Cummings realized that he had raised his voice. He took a deep breath and made an effort to soften his tone.

"I love Germany, Max, just like you do," Cummings said. "I love Cologne, Claudia's Cologne. I love Berlin and I love London. Werner's death affected Claudia and me in more ways than you can imagine. Claudia was very upset. It has driven us apart."

London, December 1944

It was a cold and misty dawn with a reddish glow in the sky. Fires were burning in adjacent buildings to the vaporized Islington pub. In the dark garden, Cummings in a flat cap and a threadbare coat was sitting in a wooden chair knocking back shots of brandy and contemplating the hellish vision of London after the bombing. Claudia stepped outside to join her husband in a winter coat pulled over her pyjamas.

"Steffi is finally asleep, Paul."

"Good, it has been a terrible night."

"There is nothing left to save, Paul. The neighbours are saying that it was a direct hit. The bomb wiped the pub off the map. No one heard it coming in."

"It was a V2, darling. The RAF is trying to destroy their bases in Germany. They are bombing us here but also the Dutch in Antwerp."

"I can't stay here any longer. I must get Steffi out of the city."

"We'll be all right, darling. The V2s aren't so frequent."

Claudia fumed observing her husband's stoic resignation in the face of this imminent danger from the sky.

"We must do something, Paul. We cannot sit around waiting for another bomb to strike."

"Come and have a drink with me, darling. It will calm your

nerves."

"All you can do is drink. You are pathetic, drinking your sorrow away."

"My dear, there is nothing we can do."

"You English are crazy. You just sit there waiting for a bomb to fall on your head. I won't allow Steffi to live a life of terror. I am packing our bags. I will call Mama."

"Please, Claudia," Cummings said.

"These bombs, they are silent killers, Paul. I am terrified for Steffi. London is a city of dust and destruction."

Claudia returned to the house, slamming the door.

Abergavenny, February 1945

"Claudia would not spend one more night in London," Cummings said. "I took them to the train that same day. They went to Dorset to stay with Claudia's parents. They are safe there away from the bombing in London. Are you still driving the staff crazy with your demands, Max?"

Z smiled as Cummings looked out the window at the garden covered in frost.

"Why did you do it, Max?"

"I tried to stab my heart, but it was not enough."

Cummings looked at the bandage on Z's chest.

"They say you put on your Luftwaffe uniform in preparation for your suicide. They say it was a superficial wound. Self-mutilation is not suicide, Max. It is just another sign of your neurotic behaviour."

Cummings paused to look at Z's gaunt demeanour. He seemed to have aged a lot since the last time he had seen him.

"Captain, I am a famous war criminal," Z said with pride.

"They want to try me like Lord Haw Haw."

"It is not my business to provide advice, Max, but I think you should hear it."

"Captain, the government wants to send me to this war crimes tribunal in Germany."

"I know that Max, but you will be risking a death sentence at a war crimes tribunal. You think we are soft on German agents in this country? We hang German agents, Max. Men, we can't turn or won't help us, we hang them. We show no mercy. When we catch William Joyce, he will die on the gallows."

"Do you listen to him on *Germany Calling*, Captain? Lord Haw Haw is still quite popular, I think."

"Of course, I do. He helps British POWs send messages to their families."

"I don't think the British can hang him, Captain. He is an American citizen and a naturalized German. He can say what he likes."

"His radio show is German propaganda and is considered to be an act of treason in this country. Mark my words, there will be no forgiveness for Lord Haw Haw. Nor will there be any forgiveness for you, Max."

"I don't want to go to a POW camp or be sent to one of those displaced persons camps in Germany."

"Your only hope of avoiding a death sentence is to write a full confession with all the details. I will take it to Major Foley. Your confession could get you special circumstances, Max."

"I am a farmer. That is all I know. Do you think a farmer like me can be a war criminal among the greatest war criminals in this world. It would be a great honour."

"It is no bloody honour, Max. It's a disgrace to be among those men. They are butchers. You are not one of them."

"You know my mother kept a picture of the Führer in the

house. Not the usual kind of picture you see everywhere. In this picture, the Führer is shaking the hand of Paul Von Hindenburg in his field marshal uniform back in '33. His head is bowed in respect for the old officer with all his medals. It's a very moving moment for us Germans."

"Yes, I have seen it."

"It had a huge impact on my family. The photograph was taken in Potsdam at the celebration of the opening of the Reichstag. You see my family always loved the Führer. He was a man who did so much for us Germans. We were very poor, you know. We were getting nothing for our potatoes so when the Führer became Chancellor, the first thing he did was fix the price of food."

"Don't go down with him, Max. He has brought terrible retribution on Germany."

Z grasped Cummings' hand.

"How is little Steffi?"

"She is fine. She talks all the time, Max. I am going to see her and her mum on the weekend before I return to London."

"Show me a photograph."

Cummings pulled a photograph of Steffi from his wallet and showed it to Z.

"What a lovely child!" Z exclaimed.

Fifty-five

Dorset 1945

On a wet evening, Cummings was dropped off at a rundown farm in the country. The sun had finally emerged from the clouds as the staff car disappeared down the muddy lane, leaving Cummings to walk up the rutted track to the house. It was a quiet evening with only the sounds of clucking chickens and distant cow bells.

Cummings picked up his bag and headed up the track to the thatched cottage. He smiled as he saw Steffi appear in the yellow light of the doorway. She took her thumb out of her mouth and stared at him. She yelled to her mother in the kitchen.

"Mama, there is a man in the lane."

Steffi ran forward to get a better look. Cummings dropped his bag and waved at her.

"Mama! It's Daddy!"

Steffi ran as fast as she could into the arms of her father. He got down on a knee and hugged the child, then looked towards the house and saw Claudia standing in the doorway. They had been separated for nearly eight weeks. He had no idea what to expect.

Claudia saw Paul in the lane embracing their daughter and her fear and longing quickly got the better of her. She ran down to join them, wrapping her arms around her husband and child.

"Paul, *Liebling*."

"*Ich habe dich vermisst, Claudia* . I missed you."

"I missed you too, Daddy."

Steffi noticed her mother's tears.

"Are you sad, Mummy?"

"Your mum is not sad. I think she is happy."

"*Ich bin glücklich*. Your daddy has come home."

Claudia kissed Paul hard on the mouth. Markus and Rosa hesitantly left the house and approached the couple in the fading light.

Fifty-six

Berlin 1973

"Everything I am telling you, Dr Terry, is highly confidential," Cummings said. "I never told you any of this, you never heard it from me. I hope you understand."

"Of course," Terry said.

"I am retiring from the service next week. I have carried this secret for quite some time, 32 years to be precise. It's been quite a burden for me and my wife, helping to maintain the lie for so many years. We cannot talk to our children about the war years."

"Yes, I can see that."

"If someone would put something in print, write a book perhaps. It might help Max, you know."

"Write a book?"

"A serious work, something solid, well referenced, irrefutable."

"Yes, I see. Something irrefutable."

"Of course, you would need a secret informant so that not a word could be traced back to me."

"A secret informant?"

"Yes, I could go to prison if it were to get out."

" I still don't understand the government's position, Paul. Why would they have been so much against Max's public confession?"

"Remember in the summer of 1942, the British government was worried that the Russians might make a separate peace with Hitler. It was a bad time. We were losing numerous supply ships on the Murmansk and Archangel run in the Russian Arctic. The war was going very badly. Suing for peace was always an option for Stalin. We were willing to do anything to keep the Russians in the war. We gave them the Baltic states. We gave them Poland. We gave them Hess."

Cummings drank the last of his beer.

"So if Max wanted to go to Nuremberg to play the fool, the Foreign Office could wash their hands of him. He would become an American problem, a Russian problem, a French problem, no longer a British problem. That's how they saw it."

"Wasn't he going to be declared unfit for trial?"

"By the end of 1945, Colonel Rees was using the schizophrenia word in his reports to describe Z's behaviour. The government was furious and warned its people to banish any use of the term in their reports to the court. They wanted Z fit for trial to appease the Russians."

Dorset 1945

Major Foley and Cummings were walking the major's black labrador in a field near the farm belonging to Claudia's parents.

"He won't make a written confession, sir," Cummings said.

"He is a good Nazi, Paul. Good Nazis don't confess. They are boy scouts and love the party line."

"I just can't accept sending him to a war crimes tribunal."

"It is not our decision. 'C' has made a full report to the Foreign Secretary. They know he is an imposter. That is all we can do."

"He could go to the newspapers to make his case."

"The government might then declare him an enemy agent and have him hanged, you know. The blame game is starting. It is not a good time to be a Nazi war criminal."

Fifty-seven

Nuremberg, October 1945

"Do you know how many persons were liquidated by Einsatz Group D under your command?"

Colonel John Amen put the question to SS-General Otto Ohlendorf, chief of *Einzatzgruppe D* in charge of eliminating Jews and communists in Ukraine.

"In the year between June 1941 and June 1942, the Einsatzkommandos reported 90,000 people liquidated," Ohlendorf said to a shocked silence in the courtroom.

In the dock, there were twenty-four German war criminals, including Rudolf Hess, sitting next to Herman Göring. Hess was reading a book and seemed distracted by the testimony.

Opposite the accused, there were eight judges (two from each Allied nation) and four prosecutors sitting at a long bench. Lord Justice Lawrence was the British president of the tribunal. Near the dock, there were a dozen white helmeted US military police providing security. There was a huge audience of newspaper reporters and the general public.

"Did that include men, women, and children?" Amen asked the witness.

"Yes," Ohlendorf replied.

"On what do you base those figures?"

"On reports sent by the *Einsatzkommandos* to the *Einsatzgruppen*."

"Did you personally supervise the mass executions of these individuals?"

"I was present at two mass executions for purposes of inspection."

"Will you explain to the tribunal how a mass execution was carried out?"

"A local *Einsatzkommando* would collect all the Jews in its area by registering them. This registration was actually performed by the Jews themselves. After the registration, they were collected at one place and from there, they were transported to the place of execution, which was as a rule an antitank ditch or a natural excavation. The executions were carried out in a military manner by firing squads."

"In what way were they transported to the place of execution?"

"They were transported in trucks and only as many as could be executed immediately. In this way, it was attempted to keep the span of time from the moment in which the victims knew what was about to happen to them until the time of their actual execution as short as possible."

"Was that your idea?"

"Yes, it was."

"What determination, if any, was made as to whether the persons were actually dead?"

"The unit leaders or the firing-squad commanders had orders to see to this and, if need be, to finish them off themselves."

"In what positions were the victims shot?"

"Standing or kneeling. Some of the unit leaders did not

carry out liquidations in the military manner, but killed the victims one by one by shooting them in the back of the neck."

"And you objected to that procedure?"

"I was against that procedure, yes."

"For what reason?"

"Because, both for the victims and for those who carried out the executions, it was psychologically an immense burden to bear."

Göring turned to Hess and the other men in the dock.

"*Verräter, verdammter Verräter.* He's a traitor, a damned traitor."

The Nazi co-defendants were startled by Göring's outburst, but not Hess, who remained unperturbed with his eyes in his book.

"Were all victims, including the men, women, and children, executed in the same manner?" Amen asked.

"Until the spring of 1942, yes. An order came from Himmler that in the future, women and children were to be killed only in gas vans."

"Will you explain to the tribunal the construction of these vans and their appearance?"

"The actual purpose of these vans could not be seen from the outside. They looked like closed trucks, and were so constructed that at the start of the motor, gas was conducted into the van, causing death in ten to fifteen minutes."

"Explain just how one of these vans was used for an execution."

"The vans were loaded with the victims and driven to the place of burial, which was usually the same as that used for the mass executions. The time needed for transportation was sufficient to ensure the death of the victims."

"How were the victims induced to enter the vans?"

"They were told they were being transported to another locality."

Two American soldiers were escorting Z from the cell block to the administration offices when they ran into *Reichsmarschall* Herman Göring coming the other way. Göring was dressed in an old grey suit and accompanied by two guards. Z stopped in the hallway and raised his arm in a Nazi salute.

"Herr Göring, Heil Hitler."

Göring was astonished by Z's salute and the insane look on his face. He broke into a laugh as the guards hauled him away. An American soldier whispered in Z's ear.

"Don't do that, man. Nazi salutes are not allowed in this prison."

"Unfortunately, I can't remember a thing. I can't even remember what happened ten days ago," Z said under the bright light in the office of the old German *Justizpalast*.

Hess sat manacled to a chair in his old Luftwaffe uniform. Colonel John Amen got up from his desk near the court reporter and the interpreter, and came around into the light.

"You mean that you can't remember what your last official position was in Germany?"

"I have no idea. It's like a fog."

Amen presented Z with a document.

"This is a handwritten document that you brought with you from England."

"I can't imagine that I was in a position to write a thing like that."

"This is your handwriting, I believe."

"I didn't have a typewriter, so I suppose it must have been written by me."

"How do you know you didn't have a typewriter?"

"Oh, just by coincidence, I can remember that."

"Your memory reaches just about where you want it to reach. Isn't that so, Mr Hess?"

Amen put the file on the table.

"Do you remember your family?"

"Yes."

"How do you remember them?"

"I have a photograph of my wife and boy with me at all times, alongside that of the Führer, of course."

"When did you last see your wife?"

"It is logical to assume that I saw Ilse before I departed."

"And your son Wolf-Rüdiger. His nickname is Buz, I believe."

"Yes. Probably the day I left."

"When did you get this idea of losing your memory?"

"I don't know. It is a fact that I don't have it now."

"I meant when did you get the idea that it would be a smart thing to lose it?"

"I don't quite understand. You mean to say that I thought it might be a good idea to lose my memory so I could deceive you?"

"Yes. That is just what I meant."

Hess remained silent for a moment.

"I don't see what benefit losing one's memory can serve."

Amen picked up his file from the desk.

"You remember Professor Haushofer, who visited us the other day. He is a very nice man, and you were his favourite student."

"Yes."

"He told me that you once read a Swedish novel in class about a student who had lost his memory and then regained it with the help of music and poetry. I think that is where you got this idea of losing your memory, isn't it?"

Z laughed out loud.

"No, certainly not. Colonel Amen, you cannot be serious."

"Why? Do you think this is funny?"

"Please, sir. Put yourself in my shoes. I won't be able to defend myself during the trial. The only instrument I have to fight with is my brain and my memory."

Amen shrugged and returned to his seat.

Fifty-eight

Z was reading a German newspaper sitting near the window in his cell. A black American soldier called his name from the prison hallway.

"Hess, I have a visitor for you."

Z went to the door with the number 125 painted on it. He squinted at the soldier in the hall.

"Sir, there is no such person as Hess here, but if you are looking for the convict in cell 125, I am your man."

The soldier grinned at the prisoner.

"You crazy old fool. They gonna hang your ass, man."

Cummings was brought down the hall, and the soldier opened the door to Z's cell.

"Hello, convict number 125."

"How are you, sir?"

"Fine. Claudia sends her best wishes."

"How is young Steffi these days?"

"She's fine and doing well in school. We have a new house in Surrey, near Guildford with a nice garden in the back. It's not that far from Mytchett. What about yourself?"

"I am fine, Paul, but it gets cold here at night and I only have this one blanket."

"I will talk to the Americans about getting you another

blanket. You look very thin. Are you eating alright?"

"Yes, the food is good."

"I have just come from a meeting with your lawyer, Dr Von Rohrscheidt. You know, he has requested a neutral medical expert from Switzerland to examine your mental fitness."

"He is not my lawyer."

"He thinks he can get you off if you are recognized as a full-blown schizophrenic. You would be repatriated and put in a mental hospital, possibly in Switzerland."

"I am not crazy, Paul."

"You could be out in a few years, Max."

Z showed no interest in becoming a mental patient in a Swiss hospital.

"What do you want me to do, Max?"

"Nothing, Paul. I look forward to pleading my case. I don't need any help from lawyers."

"I'm sorry, Max. I should have done more for you. Maybe if I had leaked your confession."

"You have done your best for me, Paul. No one could do more. I will always remember your efforts on my behalf."

"I have a visitor to meet you today, Mr Hess," Colonel Amens said. "Her name is Hildegard Fath. She worked for you as a secretary."

Hess didn't respond. He was manacled to a chair in the prison office. Amens gestured to Dr Gilbert, the American psychologist, to open the door and bring in the woman. Gilbert stepped outside briefly and brought in Hildegard Fath, a dark-haired woman in her thirties.

"*Guten Tag, Herr Hess. Ich bin Hildegard Fath.* I was your secretary in Berlin."

Fath moved closer and touched Z's arm. He looked up at her, his expression blank.

"You must remember me, sir?"

"*Nein, Fräulein.*"

"I started in your office in 1933."

"Did I work you hard, *Fräulein*?"

"No, you were always very kind to me, sir."

"I do not remember this woman, Colonel."

Fath stepped back, looking very upset.

"I am a close friend of the family, sir. You must remember me. I have pictures of your wife and child," Fath protested, showing him a photograph of his son, Buz. "Here, this will help you remember. Look at it."

Z pushed the photograph away, annoyed by this intrusion.

"No, no, no. I do not want your help."

Hildegard Fath stepped back in frustration as Amen approached.

"Thank you, Miss Fath," Amen said. "You remember this woman, don't you, sir?"

"No, sir."

"Of course he does, Miss Fath. Don't worry."

Dr Gilbert led the distressed woman out of the room and brought in an older blonde woman with an elegant air.

"This is Miss Ingeborg Sperr," Gilbert said.

Miss Sperr advanced into the light.

"*Guten Tag, Herr Hess. Ich bin Ingebord Sperr.* I was your secretary for seven years in Munich. You must remember me."

"*Fräulein Sperr*, were you happy working for me?"

"I was very happy to work for you, sir."

Z nodded patiently.

"Ilse, Buz and your brother Alfred have been to visit me. He is a lovely boy. He will be 8 years old in a few days. I mailed you photographs."

"Yes, I received them in January."

"I wrote to you many times, and you never replied. Ilse is asking to see you."

"I am anxious all the time, *Fräulein*," Z said. "Everything is so changed. I cannot remember things."

"After your flight, I spent six weeks in prison at Dachau. I suffered a great deal. I was interrogated by the Americans several times. They asked me which I preferred, an honourable enemy or a false friend?"

"What did you say?"

"A false friend, Herr Hess. I prefer a false friend."

Amen stepped forward as Miss Sperr retreated.

"Thank you, Miss Sperr. Here is a man who is not a friend at all. He is lying to us all. You remember these ladies, don't you?"

"No, sir. I never saw them before in my life."

In his prison cell, Z was reading a book as he sat on a chair near the window. He heard a voice from an American soldier at the door.

"Hess, Dr Gilbert is here to see you."

The cell door swung open and Dr Gilbert, with his round spectacles and predatory stare, appeared in the doorway. Despite his official job description as a psychologist, a major part of Gilbert's job was actually to make notes of everything the prisoners said and report back to the US prosecution team.

"How are you this morning, Herr Hess?"

"I am fine, Doctor."

"The director is worried about you. You are looking very thin."

"I am eating well, Doctor."

"Tomorrow your lawyer ,Von Rohrscheidt ,will present your case. I hear the judges will probably find you incompetent to defend yourself."

"But I am perfectly competent to defend myself."

"My bet is that it will be over for you tomorrow. You won't be a free man, but you won't be facing the death penalty. This is very good news. What do you think?"

"But I want to continue to take part in the trial, sir. It is my right to see it through to the end."

"Don't you want to be a free man, Herr Hess?" Gilbert asked with a self-satisfied smirk before calling for the guard to open the door.

Fifty-nine

November 30, 1945

"*Meine geehrte Herren Richter.* My distinguished judges. May it please the tribunal I am speaking as counsel for the defendant Rudolf Hess," Von Rohrscheidt addressed the court as Z sat alone in the dock.

"In the proceedings that have been opened against Hess, the court is to decide solely the question of whether the defendant is fit or unfit to be heard, and whether he might even be considered entirely responsible for his actions."

A quiet came over the tribunal as Lord Justice Lawrence raised a hand from the bench.

"I believe the medical experts agree that the defendant is capable of understanding the course of the proceedings," Lawrence said, "but he suffers from forgetfulness about what happened before he flew to England."

"Nothing prevents in English jurisprudence to my knowledge a trial or punishment of a person who claims to be forgetful as to what happened at the time," said the British prosecutor Major David Maxwell-Fyfe.

"Mr President, is it not true that the medical experts consider the defendant Hess incapable of defending himself?"

Von Rohrscheidt asked.

In the dock, Z listened with unusual intensity and pencilled a note for his lawyer that he gave to a white helmeted US soldier behind him.

"Surely, Herr Hess could argue that he might have been able to mount a better defence if he could remember what took place at the time," Lawrence said.

The US prosecutor Justice Robert Jackson was not having any of it and held up a copy of Dr Rees' medical report on the prisoner during his time in England.

"I have here Hess' medical report, gentlemen. As you know he has refused drugs numerous times that could have helped cure his memory loss," Jackson said. "I respectfully suggest that Herr Hess cannot stand before this court and assert that his amnesia is a defence to his being tried and, at the same time, refuse the simple medical expedients which we all agree might be useful."

"But Mr Jackson, Hess has every right to refuse forceful drug injections," Von Rohrscheidt countered. "He has a deep abhorrence of such means and has always favoured natural methods of healing."

Rohrscheidt looked down at the pencilled note handed to him by the US soldier.

"I believe my client wants to make a statement. He says he feels fit to plead and wants to tell the court himself," Von Rohrscheidt announced.

Z stood up in the box followed by a long moment of silence in the courtroom as the judges conferred.

"I understand you want to make a brief statement to the court," Lord Justice Lawrence said as the courtroom staff and the reporters looked at the gaunt war criminal in the box.

"Mr President, I would like to make the following statement

to the court," Hess read from a handwritten note. "In order that I may be allowed to continue to attend the trial and receive judgement alongside my colleagues as is my wish, and in order not to be declared unfit to plead, I submit the following declaration. From this time on, my memory is again at the disposal of the outside world."

Von Rohrscheidt looked aghast as his client destroyed his case.

"The reasons why I simulated amnesia are of a tactical nature. In fact, only my ability to concentrate is slightly impaired. On the other hand, my ability to follow the trial, to defend myself, to question witnesses, and to answer questions myself, is not impaired. I emphasize that I assume full responsibility for everything that I have done, everything I have signed, and everything that I have co-signed."

There was an uncomfortable silence in the courtroom as Von Rohrscheidt hid his face in his hands. Laughter broke out in the press box. The president rapped his gavel for silence as the newspaper reporters rushed out of the courtroom to file their reports.

Sixty

Berlin 1973

"As you know, Max got life imprisonment," Cummings said to Terry as they stood near the water, watching the ducks on the pond at the Tiergarten park. "He has been in the Spandau prison for 27 years. They should have released him years ago, back in 1966, along with Albert Speer and Baldur Von Schirach. It is crazy to keep one harmless old man locked up in an empty prison."

"And you think a book will help?" Terry asked.

"Yes, definitely. Only public pressure will help."

"Why did he make that crazy declaration at Nuremberg? He was home free. There was no way they could condemn the man."

"Max was a prodigious actor and Nuremberg was a stage for him. A world stage with the worst Nazi war criminals. He wanted to be someone, not just another displaced person, struggling to survive from day to day in post-war Germany."

"What happened to Hess' wife and child?"

"Max refused to meet Ilse and son Buz in 1946 when the prison authorities allowed family visits. His excuse was that it was beneath his dignity to have to talk to a family member through wire mesh. He didn't want to be seen in his diminished state. It wasn't until Christmas in 1969 that he finally agreed to meet Ilse and her son."

"He must have felt a lot of guilt towards the family, refusing to meet them for over 20 years," Terry said.

"I think he felt sorry for Ilse. He had duped her for so long. He couldn't delay any longer. He had to do the right thing for her son."

Berlin, November 1969

Cummings walked up to the large green door at the Spandau prison gate on Wilhelmstrasse and rang the bell. A guard opened a sliding window and asked his business. Cummings showed the guard a visitor pass and his British passport, and then entered the prison complex.

Cummings was led down numerous corridors to a cell door in the middle of the prison. An emaciated old man aged seventy-five stood near the door, waiting to embrace his old friend.

"How are you, Max?"

"I'm fine, although I feel I am getting old. How is the family?"

"Very well. I got your message. It sounded urgent."

Z looked nervous and couldn't seem to stand still.

"It's happening, Paul. Ilse and Buz are flying into Berlin on December 24 on a BEA flight to Templehof. A car will pick them up and bring them here."

"That's wonderful. You are doing the right thing. You owe them this visit."

"Yes. I think I do."

"Buz must be in his thirties. He needs to see you, to see his father."

"I have seen pictures, Paul. He is quite a big man. Did you know, he designs airports in Hamburg?"

"No, I didn't know that, Max."

"I have written to Ilse and told her not to be disturbed when she sees me. My features are not what they once were. I look a little drawn."

"You have nothing to worry about. We all change over time, Max."

Z went over to the clothes rack in the corner and selected a sports coat and a pair of brown pants. He turned to show them to Cummings.

"What do you think? The director himself got me these pants."

"The pants look good," Cummings said.

"Or maybe I should remain in my pyjamas."

Cummings smiled at the old coot, fussing with his wardrobe. He had played a role his entire life and was now dressing for the final curtain.

December 24, 1969

Ilse Hess, in her late sixties, was dressed in a two-piece suit with a white blouse and her hair swept back in a wave as she followed a guard through the corridors of the empty prison. She was accompanied by a serious-looking young man in a dark suit with a red tie.

They entered the room through a glass-panelled door to greet Z in his blue and white striped pyjamas and dressing gown. Z jumped up, eager to greet them.

"*Guten Tag, Ilse*. I kiss your hand."

"Mama, don't give him your hand," Buz whispered.

"I kiss your hand, Rudolf."

Ilse and Z observed each other in an uneasy silence.

"We don't dare shake hands, Papa. They don't allow it. How are you? How is your health?"

"I am receiving excellent medical care for my ulcer," Z said. "You know, I was very lucky. That's what the doctors are saying."

"How did it happen, Papa?"

"Some other time perhaps, Buz. It is a long story. Please tell me about your flight today."

"It's been a long time since I have flown. The last time was with you before the war," Ilse said.

"Yes, times have changed, and you have changed."

"You too, Rudolf. You have changed. Your voice is different now from how I remember it."

"How do you mean?"

"Your voice is deeper, much deeper than before, I think."

"Oh, you mean it is more manly?"

Z and Ilse laughed nervously and shared a knowing look as Buz tried to follow this exchange.

"Papa, I hardly remember you. I hope I can visit you again, so we have time to talk."

"It was a long, long time ago. You were a little boy, now you are a grown man."

Z and Ilse looked at each other in silence as Buz continued with his questions.

Sixty-one

Oberallgäu 1978

It had been a long drive from Berlin. On the road, Dr Terry had started to doubt the usefulness of this meeting in Bad Hindelang. He had written several letters, hoping for an invitation to visit. This was not something that could be discussed over the phone and a face-to-face conversation seemed the only way to get to the truth.

Arriving in the Oberallgäu mountains, he pulled off the road into a rest stop overlooking a picture-perfect Alpine valley. He took his binoculars from the car and walked to the edge of the railing to get a look at the mountains.

It was a little after midday when Terry arrived at the Bad Hindelang Gasthaus. He stepped onto the exterior terrace and greeted Ilse Hess, a vigorous woman in her seventies, well-tanned from working in her garden.

"*Guten Tag, Frau Hess.*"

"*Grüß Gott, Herr Terry.* Thank you for coming so far. I got your letters."

"What a lovely day!"

"Yes, it is very clear today and you can see the tops of the mountains. But I suspect that you have not come all the way here today to talk about the scenery."

"Yes, you are right. I am interested in your husband."

"You know I don't get many visitors at my age."

A waitress approached to take Terry's order.

"*Einen Kaffee, bitte.*"

The waitress left, and Terry turned his attention to Ilse.

"I am a surgeon, Frau Hess. I believe I mentioned it in my letter. I have worked in a lot of British hospitals in Northern Ireland where we had all kinds of horrific bullet wounds."

"Yes, I am sure they must be terrible. My husband's wounds were very serious. He had a big scar on his chest and on his back. When he had to walk uphill, he was often short of breath."

"*Ein Lungendurchschuss.* A shot through the lungs, I believe. From his military record, I learned that he was shot on August 8, 1917, but did not reach the hospital until the following day. So clearly he received no treatment for over 12 hours and perhaps as long as 24 hours. The infection must have been very bad indeed."

"Yes. I believe you are right and, of course, no antibiotics were available at that time."

The waitress returned with Terry's coffee.

"The problem with that type of gunshot is that the surgeon has to open up the wound and clean out clothing, dirt and bone debris which is sucked in by the bullet. Cleaning a wound like that leaves a nasty-looking scar."

"I believe you. He was in the hospital for four months."

"It is really quite amazing that he survived at all. It must have been touch-and-go as he fought the infection."

"He had very good doctors, I think."

"You know I examined your husband five years ago at the British Military hospital in Berlin after he had a perforated duodenal ulcer."

"Yes, I heard the ulcer caused him a lot of pain."

"I was quite surprised, you understand, to observe that your husband had no visible sign of a bullet wound on his chest. I asked him about it and he became very nervous."

Ilse picked up her cup of coffee and looked at Terry over the rim.

"Do you know what a *schlechtes Vorgefühl* means, Herr Terry? I am not sure how you say it in English.

"I think you mean a premonition or a presentiment."

"I remember distinctly the evening of Saturday May 10, 1941. The day Rudolf left in his plane. I had put Buz to bed, and I was standing in the kitchen, looking out on our garden in Harlaching, near Munich. It was a lovely spring night, but there was a cold draught from the window, so I put on my cardigan. I suddenly had this feeling, this *schlechtes Vorgefühl*, that something terrible had happened to Rudolf. I didn't know what but I was certain my life was going to change forever."

Ilse put down her cup.

"Then a day or two later, we heard the news on the radio that Rudolf had flown his plane to Scotland and Hitler was very angry at him."

"That must have been a very difficult time for you."

"Yes, it was. Everyone who worked for Rudolf was arrested. Heydrich and Bormann came after me. They thought that I had plotted with Rudolf to fly to Scotland, but I knew absolutely nothing of his plans. It was supposed to be a routine training flight. Then I received this card from Heinrich, from Heinrich Himmler. It was signed H. Himmler in his usual way with the crossed H's. It was very strange to receive a *Beileidskarte* from the *Reichsführer* of the *Schutzstaffel*."

"A *Beileidskarte* is a condolence card, no?"

"Yes. We send a *Beileidskarte* when someone has died or has had a terrible accident. It is to express our sympathies with the victim's family. No one had died. Rudolf was in Scotland. I couldn't understand it. Himmler wrote that if anything happened to me, he would make sure that my son was looked after. From that moment on, I wondered what had happened to my husband."

"I don't understand. Why did you write to him all those years?"

"I was curious. I had a young child asking about his father, so I wrote the first letter and after a long delay I received a reply from him asking about Buz. So it became a habit, reading the letters to Buz and inventing a father for my child."

Terry could only stare at Ilse.

"When did you finally tell him?"

It was as if she hadn't heard the question. She seemed confused, lost in her thoughts.

"Buz," Terry said softly, "when did you finally tell him that the man in Spandau wasn't his father?"

She turned to him and there was a streak of stubbornness and defiance in her eyes.

"I never did. I didn't have the heart to tell him. You see, it started as a game, and he so wanted to believe. I did what so many German women did at the time when the father of their child was dead or missing in action. It is sometimes easier to believe a lie."

AFTERWORD

Solid historical research went into writing this novel, which drew on the 18 journals of the warders who cared for Hess during his incarceration in Britain, W. Hugh Thomas' *The Murder of Rudolf Hess* and numerous books on the German double agent network run by MI5. This novel is based on a lot of well-known facts since Hess was in detention for some 46 years before his death in 1987.

Much of this story is true. Dr Terry's discovery of the surgical evidence proving that Hess was an imposter is based on W. Hugh Thomas' experience as a doctor at the British Military Hospital in Berlin in 1973, which is described in his book. The imposter was interned at Mytchett House where he was under constant surveillance by three enigmatic SIS companions comprised of Major Frank Foley, Captain Barnes and Lt-Colonel Wallace. The move to Mytchett was delayed while "certain technical apparatus" were tested and installed in the basement. The circumlocution was necessary because the Geneva Convention forbade electronic eavesdropping on prisoners of war. The imposter was later moved to the Maindiff Court Hospital in Abergavenny. Dr Dicks and Major Ellis Jones existed and were involved in the man's care. The Hess imposter met with Lord Chancellor Simon, Ivone Kirkpatrick, and Commander Hamilton; he was most certainly interrogated by MI5, although we don't know whether the legendary 'Tin Eye' Stephens had a go at him; he complained endlessly about being poisoned; he tried to commit suicide twice; he was drugged by the medical doctors in an attempt to improve his memory; he went to a dog race in a Welsh village; he was sent to Nuremberg and spent the rest of his days in Spandau prison in Berlin.

For those of you who still doubt the imposter theory, there was the excellent rebuttal of the New Scientist DNA report by Andrew Rosthorn in an article entitled: "Has a DNA test solved the Rudolf Hess *doppelgänger* mystery?" After the publication of the W. Hugh Thomas book in 1979, there were questions in the House of Commons as to the prisoner's identity. Still, the government brushed them aside, declaring that it had no doubt about the identity of the prisoner. The Hess family continued to maintain their belief, at least publicly, that prisoner no. 7 was Rudolf Hess. The son, Wolf-Rüdiger, known as Buz, launched an international campaign to have his father released, petitioning governments and heads of state, but to no avail. Alone among the Allied powers, the Soviets held firm and refused any modification to the terms of Hess' imprisonment.

The mystery thickened when, on August 17, 1987, the Hess imposter was strangled to death with an electrical wire by unknown assailants in a shed in the Spandau courtyard during the US occupation of the prison. The two autopsies done on the body (one British and the other German) confirmed that the man had been strangled and had not hanged himself, as suggested by the authorities. A Spandau prison nurse, Abdallah Melaouhi, who cared for Hess at the time, said he suspected Hess had been murdered. The autopsies also showed that the man had no scars from gunshot wounds in the chest area in accordance with the 1973 observation by W. Hugh Thomas.

Perhaps the most persistent evidence that Hess was a fraud came from the physical examinations of his body and his dental records. Hans Eirew, a retired Manchester orthodontist, treated prisoner no. 7 in 1950 at the Berlin Military Hospital. In a letter, he described how he had extracted a left upper molar from the prisoner. Later, Eirew had the opportunity to consult the Nazi party dental records for the real Rudolf Hess and observed that the man had lost his upper left molar teeth early, and had an artificial metal bridge in the place of the teeth. Dental records are often used to confirm the identity of the dead, and in this case, they proved that prisoner no. 7 was indeed a *doppelgänger*.

ACKNOWLEDGMENTS

I would like to thank my wife Andrée Tousignant, son Thomas Kinsey, my editor Doug Sutherland, consultants Rebecca Hennigs and Clare Dyer, Jason Enlow, Carole Beauchamp, and everyone else who believed in this adventure and provided assistance.

THE AUTHOR

Nicholas Kinsey is a Canadian / British writer and director of feature films and television dramas. He has been a successful director, scriptwriter, director of photography, film editor, and producer over a long career. He is the bestselling author of five historical novels and twenty feature and television drama screenplays. He is owner and producer at Cinegrafica Films since 2014 and writes a history blog. He lives in Quebec City, Canada.

His novels include:

Playing Rudolf Hess
An Absolute Secret
Shipwrecked Lives
Remembrance Man
White Slave: 15 Years a Barbary Slave

www.nicholaskinsey.com/
facebook @NicholasKinseyAuthor
twitter@KinseyAuthor

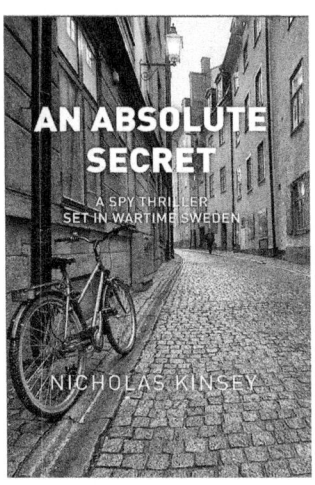

AN ABSOLUTE SECRET

A spy thriller based on real wartime intelligence operations in Sweden.

On his first assignment for MI6, British agent Peter Faye is sent to Stockholm to spy on German intelligence officer Karl-Heinz Kramer. At the British legation, he meets his new boss Bridget, a very proper, smart-as-a-whip, diplomat's daughter and immediately falls in love with her. They struggle to work together as they recruit an Austrian maid, Hanne, who works in the Kramer household. Hanne makes a copy of the key to Kramer's desk drawer and delivers secret documents to Peter and his driver Bernie who photograph them in a shed nearby. The documents are so sensitive they cause a huge commotion in London. With the help of a Swedish journalist, Peter discovers a network of Soviet moles working in British Intelligence and becomes the target of Soviet NKVD terror tactics.

"Kinsey has written a book that will comfortably sit along with the best writers of this genre. I thoroughly enjoyed this book and can wholeheartedly recommend." BookSirens

SHIPWRECKED LIVES

A NOVEL ABOUT
THE GOVERNMENT INQUIRY INTO
THE DISASTROUS SINKING OF
THE *EMPRESS OF IRELAND*

NICHOLAS KINSEY

SHIPWRECKED LIVES

The *Empress of Ireland* disaster and the cover-up.

The *Empress of Ireland* passenger liner collided with the Norwegian collier *Storstad* in the St. Lawrence River on a foggy night in May 1914, sinking in 14 minutes and claimed the lives of 1,012 people. This is the story of the survivors and the government inquiry presided over by Lord Mersey, the gruff and opinionated British jurist and politician. He had led the investigation into the *Titanic* and the later *Lusitania* disasters but was sorely tested by the *Empress* Inquiry. It tells the story of the ruined captain of the passenger liner, the woman who survived the disaster and tried unsuccessfully to claim the body of her disfigured son, the Rimouski fisherman whose job was to search the debris field for the bodies of the victims, the Norwegians who were quickly condemned by the press, the shysters and wagon-chasers who fraudulently claimed insurance policies on next of kin, and the inquiry which pitted a multinational transport industry giant against a tiny Norwegian coal-hauling firm.

"Kinsey has written a historical novel that is impossible to put down," Rosalie Grosch, www.norwegianamerican.com

REMEMBRANCE MAN

Fear and despair during the 1832 cholera epidemic

During the 1832 cholera epidemic, Paolo works for his uncle as a gravedigger in Western Ontario. At night he earns a bonus from wealthy clients as a 'remembrance man' whose job is to watch over selected graves for signs of the undead. He discovers a young woman who has been buried alive and is drawn into a terrifying story of revenge and insanity. This is a tale of murder, greed and deceit, and the breakdown of society. Family members turn against family members, friends against friends, and soon everyone is out for themselves. Cholera victims are simply abandoned on the roads, and wagons are sent around to collect the bodies and bury them in cholera pits. During these dark days, stories spread about reopening coffins in which the dead had apparently revived after burial, only to die in a futile attempt to escape. No one wanted to bury a loved one who might still be alive, which led to the habit of keeping corpses around so that the families could be sure the person had really died.

"Rarely has a novelist managed to convey more vividly the breakdown of society during a cholera epidemic."

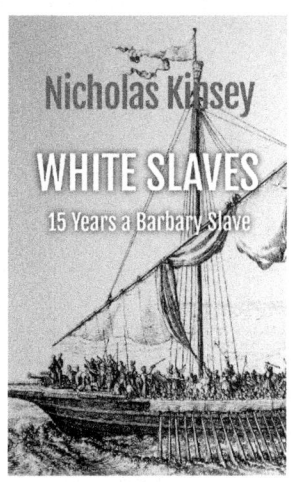

WHITE SLAVES: 15 YEARS A BARBARY SLAVE

The tragic story of the Baltimore captives

This brilliantly imagined novel tells the true story of the enslavement of the Baltimore captives and the horror of the Barbary slave trade. In the summer of 1631, the famous corsair and pirate Murad Reis attacked the peaceful fishing village of Baltimore, Ireland and seized 109 men, women and children subjecting them to a thirty-eight-day voyage down the coast of France and Spain to a life of slavery in Algiers. This is the story of that horrendous voyage and their new lives as slaves in North Africa before they were ransomed fifteen years later by the English Parliament.

"Raw, emotional and gripping are the best words for me to describe it. It was one of those "just one more chapter" scenarios at two o'clock in the morning." BookSirens

"A wonderful read!" Shonna Froebel, Canadian Bookworm

"A skillfully rendered fictional account of an obscure but fascinating slice of history." Kirkus Reviews

Printed in Dunstable, United Kingdom

64958918R00190